ON WRITING WELL

Books by William Zinsser

Any Old Place with You

Seen Any Good Movies Lately?

The City Dwellers

Weekend Guests

The Haircurl Papers

Pop Goes America

The Paradise Bit

The Lunacy Boom

On Writing Well

ON WRITING WELL

AN INFORMAL GUIDE TO WRITING NONFICTION

WILLIAM ZINSSER

1817

HARPER & ROW, PUBLISHERS

NEW YORK, HAGERSTOWN, SAN FRANCISCO, LONDON

Designed by Sidney Feinberg

Library of Congress Cataloging in Publication Data

Zinsser, William Knowlton.
   On writing well.
   Bibliography: p.
   Includes index.
   1. English language—Rhetoric. 2. Exposition
(Rhetoric) 3. Prose literature—Technique.
I. Title.
PE1429.Z5   808'.042   75-6364
ISBN 0-06-014798-9

78 79 10 9 8 7

Contents

Preface

This book grew out of a course that I teach at Yale in writing nonfiction, which in turn grew out of a long career of practicing the craft in a multitude of forms for one newspaper—the *New York Herald Tribune*—and for various magazines, mainly *Life*. It is not intended to be the last word on how to write nonfiction, or the first. I don't even claim that the book is wholly purified of the sins that it rails against with such presumptuous authority. I only know that its principles have been helpful to students, many of whom are now employed as real writers out in the real world.

It is a highly personal book—one man's opinions and prejudices. But I have included excerpts from the work of many other writers to demonstrate how they solved a particular problem. I also wanted to indicate the wide range of possibilities that are open to anyone trying to write nonfiction today, both in subject and in tone of voice. I could have chosen a different set of writers to make the same points—in fact, I have left out many of my favorites—or I could have chosen different passages from the writers whose work I did include. Who would try to pick "the best of" E. B. White? Every page of White is clean and sonorous.

My purpose is not to teach good nonfiction, or good journalism, but to teach good English that can be put to those uses. Don't assume that bad English can still be good journalism. It can't. All the writers quoted in this book were chosen because they write good English, no matter how "popular" the journal that they originally wrote for. They never talk down to the reader. They are true to themselves and to what they want to say and to how they want to say it. They are vastly dissimilar in style and in temperament, but they have all learned the one lesson that must be learned: how to control their material. You can, too.

W. Z.

New Haven, Connecticut
1976

PART I

1. The Transaction

Several years ago a school in Connecticut held "a day devoted to the arts," and I was asked if I would come and talk about writing as a vocation. When I arrived I found that a second speaker had been invited—Dr. Brock (as I'll call him), a surgeon who had recently begun to write and had sold some stories to national magazines. He was going to talk about writing as an avocation. That made us a panel, and we sat down to face a crowd of student newspaper editors and reporters, English teachers and parents, all eager to learn the secrets of our glamorous work.

Dr. Brock was dressed in a bright red jacket, looking vaguely Bohemian, as authors are supposed to look, and the first question went to him. What was it like to be a writer?

He said it was tremendous fun. Coming home from an arduous day at the hospital, he would go straight to his yellow pad and write his tensions away. The words just flowed. It was easy.

I then said that writing wasn't easy and it wasn't fun. It was hard and lonely, and the words seldom just flowed.

Next Dr. Brock was asked if it was important to rewrite. Absolutely not, he said. "Let it all hang out," and whatever form the sentences take will reflect the writer at his most natural.

I then said that rewriting is the essence of writing. I pointed out that professional writers rewrite their sentences repeatedly and then rewrite what they have rewritten. I mentioned that

E. B. White and James Thurber were known to rewrite their pieces eight or nine times.

"What do you do on days when it isn't going well?" Dr. Brock was asked. He said he just stopped writing and put the work aside for a day when it would go better.

I then said that the professional writer must establish a daily schedule and stick to it. I said that writing is a craft, not an art, and that the man who runs away from his craft because he lacks inspiration is fooling himself. He is also going broke.

"What if you're feeling depressed or unhappy?" a student asked. "Won't that affect your writing?"

Probably it will, Dr. Brock replied. Go fishing. Take a walk.

Probably it won't, I said. If your job is to write every day, you learn to do it like any other job.

A student asked if we found it useful to circulate in the literary world. Dr. Brock said that he was greatly enjoying his new life as a man of letters, and he told several luxurious stories of being taken to lunch by his publisher and his agent at Manhattan restaurants where writers and editors gather. I said that professional writers are solitary drones who seldom see other writers.

"Do you put symbolism in your writing?" a student asked me.

"Not if I can help it," I replied. I have an unbroken record of missing the deeper meaning in any story, play or movie, and as for dance and mime I have never had even a remote notion of what is being conveyed.

"I *love* symbols!" Dr. Brock exclaimed, and he described with gusto the joys of weaving them through his work.

So the morning went, and it was a revelation to all of us. At the end Dr. Brock told me he was enormously interested in my answers—it had never occurred to him that writing could be hard. I told him I was just as interested in *his* answers—it had never occurred to me that writing could be easy. (Maybe I should take up surgery on the side.)

As for the students, anyone might think that we left them bewildered. But in fact we probably gave them a broader glimpse of the writing process than if only one of us had talked. For of course there isn't any "right" way to do such intensely personal work. There are all kinds of writers and all kinds of methods, and any method that helps somebody to say what he wants to say is the right method for him.

Some people write by day, others by night. Some people need silence, others turn on the radio. Some write by hand, some by typewriter, some by talking into a tape recorder. Some people write their first draft in one long burst and then revise; others can't write the second paragraph until they have fiddled endlessly with the first.

But all of them are vulnerable and all of them are tense. They are driven by a compulsion to put some part of themselves on paper, and yet they don't just write what comes naturally. They sit down to commit an act of literature, and the self who emerges on paper is a far stiffer person than the one who sat down. The problem is to find the real man or woman behind all the tension.

For ultimately the product that any writer has to sell is not his subject, but who he is. I often find myself reading with interest about a topic that I never thought would interest me—some unusual scientific quest, for instance. What holds me is the enthusiasm of the writer for his field. How was he drawn into it? What emotional baggage did he bring along? How did it change his life? It is not necessary to want to spend a year alone at Walden Pond to become deeply involved with a man who did.

This is the personal transaction that is at the heart of good nonfiction writing. Out of it come two of the most important qualities that this book will go in search of: humanity and warmth. Good writing has an aliveness that keeps the reader reading from one paragraph to the next, and it's not a question of gimmicks to "personalize" the author. It's a question of using the English language in a way that will achieve the greatest strength and the least clutter.

Can such principles be taught? Maybe not. But most of them can be learned.

2. Simplicity

Clutter is the disease of American writing. We are a society strangling in unnecessary words, circular constructions, pompous frills and meaningless jargon.

Who really knows what the average businessman is trying to say in the average business letter? What member of an insurance or medical plan can decipher the brochure that tells him what his costs and benefits are? What father or mother can put together a child's toy—on Christmas Eve or any other eve—from the instructions on the box? Our national tendency is to inflate and thereby sound important. The airline pilot who wakes us to announce that he is presently anticipating experiencing considerable weather wouldn't dream of saying that there's a storm ahead and it may get bumpy. The sentence is too simple—there must be something wrong with it.

But the secret of good writing is to strip every sentence to its cleanest components. Every word that serves no function, every long word that could be a short word, every adverb that carries the same meaning that is already in the verb, every passive construction that leaves the reader unsure of who is doing what—these are the thousand and one adulterants that weaken the strength of a sentence. And they usually occur, ironically, in proportion to education and rank.

During the late 1960's the president of Princeton University wrote a letter to mollify the alumni after a spell of campus unrest. "You are probably aware," he began, "that we have been experiencing very considerable potentially explosive expressions of dissatisfaction on issues only partially related." He meant that the students had been hassling them about different things. As an alumnus I was far more upset by the president's syntax than by the students' potentially explosive expressions of dissatisfaction. I would have preferred the presidential approach taken by Franklin D. Roosevelt when he tried to convert into English his own government's memos, such as this blackout order of 1942:

> Such preparations shall be made as will completely obscure all Federal buildings and non-Federal buildings occupied by the Federal government during an air raid for any period of time from visibility by reason of internal or external illumination.

"Tell them," Roosevelt said, "that in buildings where they have to keep the work going to put something across the windows."

Simplify, simplify. Thoreau said it, as we are so often reminded, and no American writer more consistently practiced what he preached. Open *Walden* to any page and you will find a man saying in a plain and orderly way what is on his mind:

> I love to be alone. I never found the companion that was so companionable as solitude. We are for the most part more lonely when we go abroad among men than when we stay in our chambers. A man thinking or working is always alone, let him be where he will. Solitude is not measured by the miles of space that intervene between a man and his fellows. The really diligent student in one of the crowded hives of Cambridge College is as solitary as a dervish in the desert.

How can the rest of us achieve such enviable freedom from clutter? The answer is to clear our heads of clutter. Clear thinking becomes clear writing: one can't exist without the other. It is impossible for a muddy thinker to write good English. He may get away with it for a paragraph or two, but soon the reader will be lost, and there is no sin so grave, for he will not easily be lured back.

Who is this elusive creature, the reader? He is a person with an attention span of about twenty seconds. He is assailed on every side by forces competing for his time: by newspapers and magazines, by television and radio and stereo, by his wife and children and pets, by his house and his yard and all the gadgets that he has bought to keep them spruce, and by that most potent of competitors, sleep. The man snoozing in his chair with an unfinished magazine open on his lap is a man who was being given too much unnecessary trouble by the writer.

It won't do to say that the snoozing reader is too dumb or too lazy to keep pace with the train of thought. My sympathies are with him. If a reader is lost, it is generally because the writer has not been careful enough to keep him on the path.

This carelessness can take any number of forms. Perhaps a sentence is so excessively cluttered that the reader, hacking his way through the verbiage, simply doesn't know what it means. Perhaps a sentence has been so shoddily constructed that the reader could read it in any of several ways. Perhaps the writer has switched pronouns in mid-sentence, or has switched tenses, so the reader loses track of who is talking or when the action took place. Perhaps Sentence B is not a logical sequel to Sentence A—the writer, in whose head the connection is clear, has not bothered to provide the missing link. Perhaps the writer has used an important word incorrectly by not taking the trouble to look it up. He may think that "sanguine" and "sanguinary" mean the same thing, but the difference is a bloody big one. The reader can only infer (speaking of big differences) what the writer is trying to imply.

Faced with these obstacles, the reader is at first a remarkably tenacious bird. He blames himself—he obviously missed something, and he goes back over the mystifying sentence, or over the whole paragraph, piecing it out like an ancient rune, making guesses and moving on. But he won't do this for long. The writer is making him work too hard, and the reader will look for one who is better at his craft.

The writer must therefore constantly ask himself: What am I trying to say? Surprisingly often, he doesn't know. Then he must look at what he has written and ask: Have I said it? Is it clear to someone encountering the subject for the first time? If it's not, it is because some fuzz has worked its way into the machinery. The clear writer is a person clear-headed enough to see this stuff for what it is: fuzz.

I don't mean that some people are born clear-headed and are therefore natural writers, whereas others are naturally fuzzy and will never write well. Thinking clearly is a conscious act that the writer must force upon himself, just as if he were embarking on any other project that requires logic: adding up a laundry list or doing an algebra problem. Good writing doesn't come naturally, though most people obviously think it does. The professional writer is forever being bearded by strangers who say that they'd like to "try a little writing some time" when they retire from their real profession. Good writing takes self-discipline and, very often, self-knowledge.

Many writers, for instance, can't stand to throw anything away. Their sentences are littered with words that mean essentially the same thing and with phrases which make a point that is implicit in what they have already said. When students give me these littered sentences I beg them to select from the surfeit of words the few that most precisely fit what they want to say. Choose one, I plead, from among the three almost identical adjectives. Get rid of the unnecessary adverbs. Eliminate "in a funny sort of way" and other such qualifiers—they do no useful work.

The students look stricken—I am taking all their wonderful words away. I am only taking their superfluous words away, leaving what is organic and strong.

"But," one of my worst offenders confessed, "I never can get rid

5 --

is too dumb or too lazy to keep pace with the ~~writer's~~ train
of thought. My sympathies are ~~entirely~~ with him. ~~He's not~~
~~so dumb.~~ (If the reader is lost, it is generally because the
writer ~~of the article~~ has not been careful enough to keep
him on the ~~proper~~ path.

This carelessness can take any number of ~~different~~ forms.
Perhaps a sentence is so excessively ~~long and~~ cluttered that
the reader, hacking his way through ~~all~~ the verbiage, simply
doesn't know what *it* ~~the writer~~ means. Perhaps a sentence has
been so shoddily constructed that the reader could read it in
any of *several* ~~two or three different~~ ways. ~~He thinks he knows what~~
~~the writer is trying to say, but he's not sure.~~ Perhaps the
writer has switched pronouns in mid-sentence, or ~~perhaps he~~
has switched tenses, so the reader loses track of who is
talking ~~to whom~~ or ~~exactly~~ when the action took place. Perhaps Sentence B is not a logical sequel to Sentence A -- the
writer, in whose head the connection is ~~perfectly~~ clear, has
not *bothered to provide* ~~given enough thought to providing~~ the missing link. Perhaps the writer has used an important word incorrectly by not
taking the trouble to look it up ~~and make sure.~~ He may think
that "sanguine" and "sanguinary" mean the same thing, but
~~I can assure you that~~ (the difference is a bloody big one ~~to the~~
~~reader.~~ *The reader* ~~He~~ can only ~~try to~~ infer ~~what~~ (speaking of big differences) what the writer is trying to imply.

Faced with *these* ~~such a variety of~~ obstacles, the reader
is at first a remarkably tenacious bird. He ~~tends to~~ blame*s*
himself. ~~He~~ obviously missed something, ~~he thinks,~~ and he goes
back over the mystifying sentence, or over the whole paragraph,

6 --

piecing it out like an ancient rune, making guesses and moving
on. But he won't do this for long. ~~He will soon run out of~~
~~patience.~~ (The writer is making him work too hard ~~-- harder~~
~~than he should have to work --~~ and the reader will look for
a ~~writer~~ **one** who is better at his craft.

The writer must therefore constantly ask himself: What am
I trying to say ~~in this sentence?~~ (Surprisingly often, he
doesn't know.) ~~And~~ Then he must look at what he has ~~just~~
written and ask: Have I said it? Is it clear to someone
encountering ~~who is coming upon~~ the subject for the first time? If it's
not, ~~clear,~~ it is because some fuzz has worked its way into the
machinery. The clear writer is a person ~~who is~~ clear-headed
enough to see this stuff for what it is: fuzz.

I don't mean ~~to suggest~~ that some people are born
clear-headed and are therefore natural writers, whereas
others ~~other people~~ are naturally fuzzy and will ~~therefore~~ never write
well. Thinking clearly is **a** ~~an entirely~~ conscious act that the
writer must **force** ~~keep forcing~~ upon himself, just as if he were
embarking ~~starting out~~ on any other ~~kind of~~ project that **requires** ~~calls for~~ logic:
adding up a laundry list or doing an algebra problem ~~or playing~~
~~chess.~~ Good writing doesn't ~~just~~ come naturally, though most
people obviously think **it does.** ~~it's as easy as walking.~~ The professional

---

Two pages of the final manuscript of this chapter. Although they look
like a first draft, they have already been rewritten and retyped—like
almost every other page—four or five times. With each rewrite I try
to make what I have written tighter, stronger and more precise, elimi-
nating every element that is not doing useful work, until at last I have
a clean copy for the printer. Then I go over it once more, reading it
aloud, and am always amazed at how much clutter can still be profit-
ably cut.

of anything—you should see my room." (I didn't take him up on the offer.) "I have two lamps where I only need one, but I can't decide which one I like better, so I keep them both." He went on to enumerate his duplicated or unnecessary objects, and over the weeks ahead I went on throwing away his duplicated and unnecessary words. By the end of the term—a term that he found acutely painful—his sentences were clean.

"I've had to change my whole approach to writing," he told me. "Now I have to *think* before I start every sentence and I have to *think* about every word." The very idea amazed him. Whether his room also looked better I never found out. I suspect that it did.

3. Clutter

Fighting clutter is like fighting weeds—the writer is always slightly behind. New varieties sprout overnight, and by noon they are part of American speech. It only takes a John Dean testifying on TV to have everyone in the country saying "at this point in time" instead of "now."

Consider all the prepositions that are routinely draped onto verbs that don't need any help. Head up. Free up. Face up to. We no longer head committees. We head them up. We don't face problems anymore. We face up to them when we can free up a few minutes. A small detail, you may say—not worth bothering about. It *is* worth bothering about. The game is won or lost on hundreds of small details. Writing improves in direct ratio to the number of things we can keep out of it that shouldn't be there. "Up," in "free up," shouldn't be there. It's not only unnecessary; it's silly. Can we picture anything being freed *up?* The writer of clean English must examine every word that he puts on paper. He will find a surprising number that don't serve any purpose.

Take the adjective "personal," as in "a personal friend of mine," "his personal feeling" or "her personal physician." It is typical of the words that can be eliminated nine times out of ten. The personal friend has come into the language to distinguish him from the business friend, thereby debasing not only language but friendship. Someone's feeling *is* his personal feeling—that's what "his" means. As for the personal physician, he is that man so often summoned to the dressing room of a stricken actress so that she won't have to be treated by the impersonal physician assigned to the theater. Someday I'd like to see him identified as "her doctor."

Or take those curious intervals of time like the short minute. "Twenty-two short minutes later she had won the final set." Minutes are minutes, physicians are physicians, friends are friends. The rest is clutter.

Clutter is the laborious phrase which has pushed out the short word that means the same thing. These locutions are a drag on energy and momentum. Even before John Dean gave us "at this point in time," people had stopped saying "now." They were saying "at the present time," or "currently," or "presently" (which means "soon"). Yet the idea can always be expressed by "now" to mean the immediate moment ("now I can see him"), or by "today" to mean the historical present ("today prices are high"), or simply by the verb "to be" ("it is raining"). There is no need to say "at the present time we are experiencing precipitation."

Speaking of which, we are experiencing considerable difficulty getting *that* word out of the language now that it has lumbered in. Even your dentist will ask if you are experiencing any pain. If he were asking one of his own children he would say, "Does it hurt?" He would, in short, be himself. By using a more pompous phrase in his professional role he not only sounds more important; he blunts the painful edge of truth. It is the language of the airline stewardess demonstrating the oxygen mask that will drop down if the plane should somehow run out of air. "In the extremely unlikely possibility that the aircraft should experience such an eventuality," she begins—a phrase so oxygen-depriving in itself that we are prepared for any disaster, and even gasping death shall lose its sting.

Clutter is the ponderous euphemism that turns a slum into a depressed socioeconomic area, a salesman into a marketing representative, a dumb kid into an underachiever and a bad kid into a pre-delinquent. (The Albuquerque public schools announced a program for "delinquent and pre-delinquent boys.")

Clutter is the official language used by the American corporation—in the news release and the annual report—to hide its mistakes. When a big company recently announced that it was "decentralizing its organizational structure into major profit-centered businesses" and that "corporate staff services will be aligned under two senior vice-presidents" it meant that it had had a lousy year.

Clutter is the language of the interoffice memo ("the trend to mosaic communication is reducing the meaningfulness of concern about whether or not demographic segments differ in their tolerance of periodicity") and the language of computers ("we are offering functional digital programming options that have built-in parallel reciprocal capabilities with compatible third-generation contingencies and hardware").

Clutter is the language of the Pentagon throwing dust in the eyes of the populace by calling an invasion a "reinforced protective reaction strike" and by justifying its vast budgets on the need for "credible second-strike capability" and "counterforce deterrence." How can we grasp such vaporous doubletalk? As George Orwell pointed out in "Politics and the English Language," an essay written thirty years ago but cited with amazing frequency during the Vietnam years of Johnson and Nixon, "In our time, political speech and writing are largely the defense of the indefensible. . . . Thus political language has to consist largely of euphemism, question-begging and sheer cloudy vagueness." Orwell's warning that clutter is not just a nuisance but a deadly tool did not turn out to be inoperative. By the 1960's his words had come true in America.

I could go on quoting examples from various fields—every profession has its growing arsenal of jargon to fire at the layman and hurl him back from its walls. Recently I received a brochure from a foundation which used the verb "potentialize." But the list would be depressing and the lesson tedious. The point of raising it now is to serve notice that clutter is the enemy, whatever form it takes. It slows the reader and robs the writer of his personality, making him seem pretentious.

Beware, then, of the long word that is no better than the short word: "numerous" (many), "facilitate" (ease), "individual" (man or woman), "remainder" (rest), "initial" (first), "implement" (do), "sufficient" (enough), "attempt" (try), "referred to as" (called), and hundreds more. Beware, too, of all the slippery new fad words for which the language already has equivalents: overview and quantify, optimize and maximize, parameter and interpersonal, input and throughput, peer group and paradigm, public sector and private sector. Avoid trendy words like "trendy." They are all weeds that will smother what you write.

Nor are all the weeds as obvious as these. Once alerted, anybody can see that compatible third-generation contingencies and reinforced protective reaction strikes are heavy weights to attach to any sentence. More insidious are the little growths of perfectly ordinary words with which we explain how we propose to go about our explaining, or which inflate a simple preposition or conjunction into a whole windy phrase.

"I might add," "It should be pointed out," "It is interesting to note that"—how many sentences begin with these dreary clauses announcing what the writer is going to do next? If you might add, add it. If it should be pointed out, point it out. If it is interesting to note, *make* it interesting. Being told that something is interesting is the surest way of tempting the reader to find it dull; are we not all stupefied by what follows when someone says, "This will interest you"? As for the inflated prepositions and conjunctions, they are the innumerable phrases like "with the possible exception of" (except), "for the reason that" (because), "he totally lacked the ability to" (he couldn't), "she was unable to give any information beyond the fact that" (she said).

Clutter takes more forms than you can shake twenty sticks at. Prune it ruthlessly. Be grateful for everything that you can throw away. Re-examine each sentence that you put on paper. Is every word doing new and useful work? Can any thought be expressed with more economy? Is anything pompous or pretentious or faddish? Are you hanging on to something useless just because you think it's beautiful? Remember Thoreau:

> Our life is frittered away by detail. . . . Instead of a million count half-a-dozen, and keep your accounts on your thumb-nail. . . . Let us spend one day as deliberately as Nature and not be thrown off the track by every nutshell and mosquito's wing that falls on the rails.

> Simplify, simplify.

4. Style

So much for early warnings about the bloated monsters that lie in ambush for the writer trying to put together a clean English sentence.

"But," you may say, "if I eliminate everything that you think is clutter and strip every sentence to its barest bones, will there be anything left of me?"

The question is a fair one and the fear entirely natural. Simplicity carried to its extreme might seem to point to a style where the sentences are little more sophisticated than "Dick likes Jane" and "See Spot run."

I'll answer the question first on the level of mere carpentry. Then I'll get to the larger issue of who the writer is and how to preserve his or her identity.

Few people realize how badly they write. Nobody has shown them how much excess or murkiness has crept into their style and how it obstructs what they are trying to say. If you give me an article that runs to eight pages and I tell you to cut it to four, you'll howl and say it can't be done. Then you will go home and do it, and it will be infinitely better. After that comes the hard part: cutting it to three.

The point is that you have to strip down your writing before you can build it back up. You must know what the essential tools are and what job they were designed to do. If I may belabor the metaphor of carpentry, it is first necessary to be able to saw wood neatly and to drive nails. Later you can bevel the edges or add elegant finials, if that is your taste. But you can never forget that you are practicing a craft that is based on certain principles. If the nails are weak, your house will collapse. If your verbs are weak and your syntax is rickety, your sentences will fall apart.

I'll grant that various nonfiction writers like Tom Wolfe and Norman Mailer and Hunter Thompson have built some remarkable houses in the past decade. But these are writers who spent years learning their craft, and when at last they raised their fanciful turrets and hanging gardens, to the surprise of all of us who never dreamed of such ornamentation, they knew what they were doing. Nobody becomes Tom Wolfe overnight, not even Tom Wolfe.

First, then, learn to hammer in the nails, and if what you build is sturdy and serviceable, take satisfaction in its plain strength.

But you will be impatient to find a "style"—to embellish the plain words so that readers will recognize you as someone special. You will reach for gaudy similes and tinseled adjectives, as if "style" were something you could buy at a style store and drape onto your words in bright decorator colors. (Decorator colors are the colors that decorators come in.) Resist this shopping expedition: there is no style store.

Style is organic to the person doing the writing, as much a part of him as his hair, or, if he is bald, his lack of it. Trying to add style is like adding a toupée. At first glance the formerly bald man looks young and even handsome. But at second glance—and with a toupée there is always a second glance—he doesn't look quite right. The problem is not that he doesn't look well groomed; he does, and we can only admire the wigmaker's almost perfect skill. The point is that he doesn't look like himself.

This is the problem of the writer who sets out deliberately to garnish his prose. You lose whatever it is that makes you unique. The reader will usually notice if you are putting on airs. He wants the person who is talking to him to sound genuine. Therefore a fundamental rule is: be yourself.

No rule, however, is harder to follow. It requires the writer to do two things which by his metabolism are impossible. He must relax and he must have confidence.

Telling a writer to relax is like telling a man to relax while being prodded for a possible hernia, and, as for confidence, he is a bundle of anxieties. See how stiffly he sits at his typewriter, glaring at the paper that awaits his words, chewing the eraser on the pencil that is so sharp because he has sharpened it so many times. A writer will do anything to avoid the act of writing. I can testify from my newspaper days that the number of trips made to the watercooler per reporter-hour far exceeds the body's known need for fluids.

What can be done to put the writer out of these miseries? Unfortunately, no cure has yet been found. I can only offer the consoling thought that you are not alone. Some days will go better than others; some will go so badly that you will despair of ever writing again. We have all had many of these days and will have many more.

Still, it would be nice to keep the bad days to a minimum, which brings me back to the matter of trying to relax.

As I said earlier, the average writer sets out to commit an act of literature. He thinks that his article must be of a certain length or it won't seem important. He thinks how august it will look in print. He thinks of all the people who will read it. He thinks that it must have the solid weight of authority. He thinks that its style must dazzle. No wonder he tightens: he is so busy thinking of his awesome responsibility to the finished article that he can't even start. Yet he vows to be worthy of the task. He will do it—by God!—and, casting about for heavy phrases that would never occur to him if he weren't trying so hard to make an impression, he plunges in.

Paragraph 1 is a disaster—a tissue of ponderous generalities that seem to have come out of a machine. No *person* could have written them. Paragraph 2 is not much better. But Paragraph 3 begins to have a somewhat human quality, and by Paragraph 4 the writer begins to sound like himself. He has started to relax.

It is amazing how often an editor can simply throw away the first three or four paragraphs of an article and start with the paragraph where the writer begins to sound like himself. Not only are the first few paragraphs hopelessly impersonal and ornate; they also don't really say anything. They are a self-conscious attempt at a fancy introduction, and none is necessary.

A writer is obviously at his most natural and relaxed when he writes in the first person. Writing is, after all, a personal transaction between two people, even if it is conducted on paper, and the transaction will go well to the extent that it retains its humanity. Therefore I almost always urge people to write in the first person —to use "I" and "me" and "we" and "us." They usually put up a fight.

"Who am I to say what *I* think?" they ask. "Or what *I* feel?"

"Who are you *not* to say what you think?" I reply. "There's only one you. Nobody else thinks or feels in exactly the same way."

"But no one cares about my opinions," they say. "It would make me feel conspicuous."

"They'll care if you tell them something interesting," I say, "and tell them in words that come naturally."

Nevertheless, getting writers to use "I" is seldom easy. They think they must somehow earn the right to reveal their emotions or their deepest thoughts. Or that it is immodest. Or that it is undignified—a fear that hobbles the academic world. Hence the professorial use of "one" ("One finds oneself not wholly in accord with Dr. Maltby's view of the human condition") and of the impersonal "it is" ("It is to be hoped that Professor Felt's essay will find the wider audience that it most assuredly deserves"). These are arid constructions. "One" is a pedantic fellow—I've never wanted to meet him. I want a professor with a passion for his subject to tell me why it fascinates *him.*

Sell yourself, and your subject will exert its own appeal. Believe in your own identity. Proceed with confidence, generating it, if necessary, by pure willpower. Writing is an act of ego and you might as well admit it. Use its energy to keep yourself going.

5. The Audience

Soon after you confront this matter of preserving your identity, another question will occur to you: "Who am I writing for?"

It is a fundamental question and it has a fundamental answer: you are writing for yourself. Don't try to visualize the great mass audience. There is no such audience—every reader is a different person. Don't try to guess what sort of thing editors might want to publish or what you think the country is in a mood to read. Editors and readers don't know what they want to read until they read it. Besides, they're always looking for something new.

Don't worry about whether the reader will "get it" if you indulge a sudden impulse for humor or nonsense. If it amuses you in the act of writing, put it in. (It can always be taken out later, but only you can put it in.) You are writing primarily to entertain yourself, and if you go about it with confidence you will also entertain the readers who are worth writing for. If you lose the dullards back in the dust, that's where they belong.

I realize that I have raised what may seem to be a paradox. Earlier I warned that the reader is an impatient bird, perched on the thin edge of distraction or sleep. Now I am saying that you must write for yourself and not be gnawed by constant worry over whether he is tagging along behind.

I'm talking about two different problems. One is craft, the other is attitude. The first is a question of mastering a precise skill; the second is a question of how you use that skill to express your personality.

In terms of craft, there is no excuse for losing the reader through sloppy workmanship. If he drowses off in the middle of your article because you have been careless about a technical detail, the fault is entirely yours. But on the larger issue of whether the reader likes you, or likes what you are saying, or how you are saying it, or agrees with it, or feels an affinity for your sense of humor or your vision of life, don't give him a moment's worry. You are who you are, he is who he is, and either you will get along or you won't.

Perhaps this still seems like a paradox—or at least an impossible mental act to perform. How can you think carefully about not losing the reader and still be so carefree about his opinion that you will be yourself? I can only assure you that they are two distinct processes.

First, work hard to master the tools. Simplify, prune and strive for order. Think of this as a mechanical act and soon your sentences will become cleaner. The act will never become as mechanical as, say, shaving—you will always have to think about the various ways in which the tools can be used. But at least your sentences will be grounded in solid principles, and your chances of losing the reader will be smaller.

Think of the other process as a creative act—the expressing of who you are. Relax and say what you want to say. And since style is who you are, you only need to be true to yourself to find it gradually emerging from under the accumulated clutter and debris, growing more distinctive every day. Perhaps the style won't solidify for several years as *your* style, *your* voice—and, in fact, it shouldn't. Just as it takes time to find yourself as a person, it takes time to find yourself as a stylist, and even then, inevitably, your style will change as you grow older.

But whatever your age, be yourself when you write. Many old men still write with the zest that they had in their twenties or early thirties; obviously their ideas are still young. Other old writers ramble and repeat themselves; their style is the tip-off that they have turned into redundant bores. Many college students write as if they were desiccated alumni thirty years out.

Let's look at a few writers to see the sheer pleasure with which they put onto paper their passions and their crotchets, not caring whether the reader shares them or not. The first excerpt is from "The Hen (An Appreciation)," written by E. B. White in 1944 at the height of World War II:

Chickens do not always enjoy an honorable position among city-bred people, although the egg, I notice, goes on and on. Right now the hen is in favor. The war has deified her and she is the darling of the home front, feted at conference tables, praised in every smoking car, her girlish ways and curious habits the topic of many an excited husbandryman to whom yesterday she was a stranger without honor or allure.

My own attachment to the hen dates from 1907, and I have been faithful to her in good times and bad. Ours has not always been an easy relationship to maintain. At first, as a boy in a carefully zoned suburb, I had neighbors and police to reckon with; my chickens had to be as closely guarded as an underground newspaper. Later, as a man in the country, I had my old friends in town to reckon with, most of whom regarded the hen as a comic prop straight out of vaudeville. . . . Their scorn only increased my devotion to the hen. I remained loyal, as a man would to a bride whom his family received with open ridicule. Now it is my turn to wear the smile, as I listen to the enthusiastic cackling of urbanites, who have suddenly taken up the hen socially and who fill the air with their newfound ecstasy and knowledge and the relative charms of the New Hampshire Red and the Laced Wyandotte. You would think, from their nervous cries of wonder and praise, that the hen was hatched yesterday in the suburbs of New York, instead of in the remote past in the jungles of India.

To a man who keeps hens, all poultry lore is exciting and endlessly fascinating. . . . Every spring I settle down with my farm journal and read, with the same glazed expression on my face, the age-old story of how to prepare a brooder house—as a housemaid might read, with utter absorption, an article on how to make a bed. . . .

Now there's a man writing about a subject that I have absolutely no interest in. Yet I enjoy this piece thoroughly. I like the simple beauty of its style. I like the rhythms, the unexpected but refreshing words ("deified," "allure," "cackling"), the specific details like the Laced Wyandotte and the brooder house. But mainly what I like is that this is a man telling me unabashedly about a love affair with poultry that goes back to 1907. It is written with humanity and warmth, and after three paragraphs I know quite a lot about what sort of man this hen-lover is.

Or take a writer who is almost White's opposite in terms of style, who relishes the opulent word for its very opulence and does not deify the simple sentence. Yet they are brothers in holding firm opinions and saying what they think. This is H. L. Mencken reporting on the "Monkey Trial"—the trial of John Scopes, the young teacher who taught the theory of evolution in his Tennessee classroom—in the summer of 1925:

It was hot weather when they tried the infidel Scopes at Dayton, Tenn., but I went down there very willingly, for I was eager to see something of evangelical Christianity as a going concern. In the big cities of the Republic, despite the endless efforts of consecrated men, it is laid up with a wasting disease. The very Sunday-school superintendents, taking jazz from the stealthy radio, shake their fire-proof legs; their pupils, moving into adolescence, no longer respond to the proliferating hormones by enlisting for missionary service in Africa, but resort to necking instead. Even in Dayton, I found,

though the mob was up to do execution on Scopes, there was
a strong smell of antinomianism. The nine churches of the
village were all half empty on Sunday, and weeds choked
their yards. Only two or three of the resident pastors managed
to sustain themselves by their ghostly science; the rest had
to take orders for mail-order pantaloons or work in the adjacent strawberry fields; one, I heard, was a barber. . . .
Exactly twelve minutes after I reached the village I was taken
in tow by a Christian man and introduced to the favorite
tipple of the Cumberland Range; half corn liquor and half
Coca-Cola. It seemed a dreadful dose to me, but I found that
the Dayton illuminati got it down with gusto, rubbing their
tummies and rolling their eyes. I include among them the
chief local proponents of the Mosaic cosmogony. They were
all hot for Genesis, but their faces were too florid to belong
to teetotalers, and when a pretty girl came tripping down
the main street, they reached for the places where their neck-
ties should have been with all the amorous enterprise of
movie stars. . . .

This is pure Mencken, both in its surging momentum and in its
irreverence. At almost any page where you open one of his books
he is saying something sure to outrage the professed pieties of his
countrymen. The sanctity in which Americans bathed their heroes,
their churches and their edifying laws—especially Prohibition—
was a well of hypocrisy for him that never even came close to
drying up. Some of his heaviest ammunition he hurled at Presidents and politicians—his portrait of "The Archangel Woodrow"
still scorches the pages after half a century—and as for Christian
believers and clerical folk in general, they turn up unfailingly as
mountebanks and boobs.

It may seem a miracle that Mencken could get away with such
heresies in the 1920's, when hero-worship was an American religion and the self-righteous wrath of the Bible Belt oozed from
coast to coast. In fact, not only did he get away with it; he was

the most revered and influential journalist of his generation. The impact that he made on subsequent writers of nonfiction is beyond measuring, and even now his topical pieces seem as fresh as if they were written yesterday.

The secret of his popularity—aside from his pyrotechnical use of the American language—was that he was obviously writing for himself and didn't ever worry over what the reader might think. It wasn't necessary to share his prejudices to enjoy seeing them expressed with such mirthful abandon. Mencken was never timid or evasive. He didn't kowtow to the reader or curry his favor. It takes courage to be such a writer, but it is out of such courage that revered and influential journalists are born.

Lest I seem to be choosing my writers only from the safe and distant past, let me close with a shot straight into the veins from a 1971 book, *Fear and Loathing in Las Vegas*, by Hunter S. Thompson. We find our author stopping by the roadside in his drive across Nevada to cover the National District Attorneys' Conference on Narcotics and Dangerous Drugs. The irony of this particular reporter assigned to this particular conference is rich enough to out-Mencken Mencken. If Thompson has consumed only a fraction of the stuff that he claims to swallow, his brain must be pure watermelon.

Luckily, nobody bothered me while I ran a quick inventory on the kit-bag. The stash was a hopeless mess, all churned together and half-crushed. Some of the mescaline pellets had disintegrated into a reddish-brown powder, but I counted about 35 or 40 still intact. My attorney had eaten all the reds, but there was quite a bit of speed left . . . no more grass, the coke bottle was empty, one acid blotter, a nice brown lump of opium hash and six loose amyls . . . Not enough for anything serious, but a careful rationing of mescaline would probably get us through the four-day Drug Conference.

On the outskirts of Vegas I stopped at a neighborhood pharmacy and bought two quarts of Gold tequila, two fifths of

Chivas Regal and a pint of ether. I was tempted to ask for some amyls. My angina pectoris was starting to act up. But the druggist had the eyes of a mean Baptist hysteric. I told him I needed the ether to get the tape off my legs, but by that time he'd already rung the stuff up and bagged it.

I wondered what he would say if I asked him for $22 worth of Romilar and a tank of nitrous oxide. Probably he would have sold it to me. Why not? Free enterprise . . . give the public what it needs—especially this bad-sweaty, nervous-talkin' fella with tape all over his legs and this terrible cough, along with angina pectoris and these godawful aneuristic flashes every time he gets in the sun. I mean, this fella was in bad shape, officer. How the hell was I to know he'd walk straight out to his car and start abusing those drugs?

Well, there's a man writing for himself and not looking over his shoulder to see if the reader is clucking his tongue. Whether he is writing the exact truth—or has raised it a few notches to make a point about hypocrisy and greed in modern America—is not the point. The point is that he is writing well, and with humor, an acidhead Mencken reincarnated for the 1970's.

So let us leave Hunter Thompson popping amyls into his Chivas Regal on the outskirts of Las Vegas and tiptoe away into the setting sun.

6. Words

There is a kind of writing that might be called journalese, and it is the death of freshness in anybody's style. It is the common currency of newspapers and of magazines like *Time*—a mixture of cheap words, made-up words and clichés which have become so pervasive that a writer can hardly help using them automatically. You must fight these phrases off or you will sound like every hack who sits down at a typewriter. In fact, you will never make your mark as a writer unless you develop a respect for words and a curiosity about their shades of meaning that is almost obsessive. The English language is rich in strong and supple words. Take the time to root around and find the ones you want.

What is "journalese"? It is a quilt of instant words patched together out of other parts of speech. Adjectives are used as nouns ("greats," "notables"). Nouns are used as adjectives ("top officials," "health reasons") or extended into adjectives ("insightful"). Nouns are used as verbs ("to host"), or they are chopped off to form verbs ("enthuse," "emote"), or they are padded to form verbs ("beef up," "put teeth into").

This is a world where eminent people are "famed" and their associates are "staffers," where the future is always "upcoming" and someone is forever "firing off" a note. Nobody in *Time* has merely sent a note or a memo or a telegram in years. Famed

Diplomat Henry Kissinger, who hosts foreign notables to beef up the morale of top State Department staffers, sits down and fires off a lot of notes. Notes that are fired off are always fired in anger and from a sitting position.

Here, for example, is a *Time* article of several years ago that is hard to match for sheer fatigue:

> Last February, Plainclothes Patrolman Frank Serpico and two other New York City policemen knocked at the door of a suspected Brooklyn heroin pusher. When the door opened a crack, Serpico shouldered his way in only to be met by a .22-cal. pistol slug crashing into his face. Somehow he survived, although there are still buzzing fragments in his head, causing dizziness and permanent deafness in his left ear. Almost as painful is the suspicion that he may well have been set up for the shooting by other policemen. For Serpico, 35, has been waging a lonely, four-year war against the routine and endemic corruption that he and others claim is rife in the New York City police department. His efforts are now sending shock waves through the ranks of New York's finest. . . . Though the impact of the commission's upcoming report has yet to be felt, Serpico has little hope that anything will really change. . . .

The upcoming report has yet to be felt because it is still upcoming, and as for the "permanent deafness," it is still a little early to tell. And what makes those buzzing fragments buzz? I would have thought that by now only the head would be buzzing.

But apart from these lazinesses of logic, what makes the story so infinitely tired is the failure of the writer to reach for anything but the nearest cliché. "Shouldered his way," "only to be met," "crashing into his face," "waging a lonely war," "corruption that is rife," "sending shock waves"—these dreary phrases constitute journalese at its worst and writing at its most banal. We know just what to expect. No surprise awaits us in the form of a bizarre word, an oblique look. We are in the hands of a hack and we know it right away.

Don't let yourself get in this position. The only way to fight it is to care deeply about words. If you find yourself writing that someone recently "enjoyed" a spell of illness or that a business has been "enjoying" a slump, stop and think how much they really enjoyed it. Notice the decisions that other writers make in their choice of words and be finicky about the ones that you select from the vast supply. The race in writing is not to the swift but to the original.

In contrast to the lonely Serpico, here is how *Life* led its issue of November 1, 1968, which went to press only forty-eight hours after the surprise announcement that Mrs. Kennedy would marry Mr. Onassis. The magazine assigned the article to its best writer, Paul O'Neil, who began his story—adjacent to a color photograph of Skorpios—like this:

> But look carefully at this island in its indigo sea; observe the yacht with the golden bathtub spigots and 42 telephones; see the swimming pool; see the scarred hill where the castle will be built and while doing so think of the money piled up by the little fellow in dark glasses who owns it—one thousand million dollars. Ladies . . . ladies . . . you've had a week to be scandalized, but now we must insist that you cease sputtering and be serious—those of you over 30, at any rate, who know husbands are to be endured. And gentlemen . . . we're all carnivores here although you need not say so aloud. Are there any of us who really suspect that Jackie is not capable of enormous satisfaction at a union so rich in drama, creature comfort, power, sudden independence of social constraint— and the sweet knowledge of breast-heaving by a million indignant and defeated females—or that Onassis is not bursting with pride at his bauble of baubles?

If the story contains almost no substance (and it doesn't), it is because O'Neil had to write it in little more than a day, working only with fragmentary cables from Greece and with old clippings about the new bridegroom. Nevertheless he gave the reader a touch of elegance and a sense that, whatever the next sentence might bring, it wouldn't be like anyone else's.

So in learning to write nonfiction, make a habit of reading what is being written today and what has been written before. But cultivate the best writers. Don't assume that because an article is in a newspaper or a magazine it must be good. Lazy editing is endemic to our papers, and writers who use clichés by reflex are likely to work for editors who have seen so many clichés that they no longer even recognize them as they go limping by.

Also get in the habit of using dictionaries. My favorite for handy use is *Webster's New Collegiate*, based on the Second Edition of *Webster's New International Dictionary*, though, like all word freaks, I own many bigger dictionaries which will reward me in their own fashion when I am on some more specialized search.

If you have any doubt of what a word means, look it up. Learn its etymology and notice what curious branches its original root has put forth. See if it has any other meanings that you didn't know it had. Master the small gradations between words that seem to be synonyms. What is the difference between "cajole," "wheedle," "blandish" and "coax"? An excellent guide to these nuances is *Webster's Dictionary of Synonyms*.

And don't scorn that bulging grab-bag, *Roget's Thesaurus*. It's easy to regard the book as hilarious. Look up "villain," for example, and you will be awash in such rascality as only a lexicographer could conjure back from centuries of iniquity, obliquity, depravity, knavery, profligacy, frailty, flagrancy, infamy, immorality, corruption, wickedness, wrongdoing, backsliding and sin. You will find rogues and wretches, ruffians and riffraff, miscreants and malefactors, reprobates and rapscallions, hooligans and hoodlums, scamps and scapegraces, scoundrels and scalawags, jezebels and jades. You will find adjectives to fit them all (foul and fiendish, devilish and diabolical), and adverbs, and verbs to describe how the wrongdoers do their wrong, and cross-references leading to still other thickets of venality and vice. Still, there is no better friend to have around to nudge the memory than Roget. It saves you the time of rummaging in your own memory—that network of overloaded grooves—to find the word that is right on the tip of your tongue, where it doesn't do you any good. The *Thesaurus* is to the writer what a rhyming dictionary is to the songwriter—a reminder of all the choices—and you should use it with gratitude. If, having found the scalawag and the scapegrace, you want to know how they differ, *then* go to the dictionary.

Also bear in mind, when you are choosing words and stringing them together, how they sound. This may seem absurd: readers read with their eyes. But actually they hear what they are reading—in their inner ear—far more than you realize. Therefore such matters as rhythm and alliteration are vital to every sentence. A typical example—maybe not the best, but undeniably the nearest —is the preceding paragraph. Obviously I enjoyed making a certain arrangement of my ruffians and riffraff, my hooligans and hoodlums, and the reader enjoyed it, too—far more than if I had given him a mere list. He enjoyed not only the arrangement but the effort to entertain him. He wasn't enjoying it, however, with his eyes. He was enjoying it mainly in his ear.

E. B. White makes the case cogently in *The Elements of Style* (the best book on writing that I know) when he suggests trying to rearrange any phrase that has survived for a century or two, such as Thomas Paine's "These are the times that try men's souls":

> Times like these try men's souls.
> How trying it is to live in these times!
> These are trying times for men's souls.
> Soulwise, these are trying times.

Paine's phrase is like poetry and the other four are like oatmeal, which, of course, is the divine mystery of the creative process. Yet the good writer of prose must be part poet, always listening

to what he writes. E. B. White continues across the years to be my
favorite stylist because I am so conscious of being with a man
who cares in his bones about the cadences and sonorities of the
language. I relish (in my ear) the pattern that his words make
as they fall into a sentence. I try to surmise how in rewriting the
sentence he reassembled it to end with a phrase that will momentarily linger, or how he chose one word over another because he
was after a certain emotional weight. It is the difference between,
say, "serene" and "tranquil"—one so soft, the other strangely disturbing because of the unusual "n" and "q."

Listen to how White begins his book *Here Is New York*:

> On any person who desires such queer prizes, New York
> will bestow the gift of loneliness and the gift of privacy. It
> is this largess that accounts for the presence within the city's
> walls of a considerable section of the population; for the
> residents of Manhattan are to a large extent strangers who
> have pulled up stakes somewhere and come to town, seeking
> sanctuary or fulfillment or some greater or lesser grail. The
> capacity to make such dubious gifts is a mysterious quality
> of New York. It can destroy an individual, or it can fulfill
> him, depending a good deal on luck. No one should come to
> New York to live unless he is willing to be lucky.

Don't be deceived by the simplicity of the paragraph. I
wouldn't be surprised if White took a week to write and rewrite
it. The first sentence is a gem; so is the last. The mingling of
long Latin words like "population" and "sanctuary" with such
colloquialisms as "pulled up stakes" and "a good deal" is a
deliberate balancing act—the writer wants to use graceful words
and still be himself, talking to the reader naturally. The phrase
"some greater or lesser grail" is positively lyrical and its position
at the end of a sentence no accident.

Such considerations of sound and rhythm should be woven
through every aspect of what you write. If all your sentences
move at the same plodding gait, which even you recognize as

deadly but don't know how to cure, read them aloud. You will begin to hear where the trouble lies. See if you can gain variety by reversing the order of a sentence, by substituting a word that has freshness or oddity, by altering the length of your sentences so that they don't all sound as if they came out of the same computer. An occasional short sentence can carry a tremendous punch. It stays in the reader's ear.

Remember, then, that words are the only tools that you will be given. Learn to use them with originality and care. Value them for their strength and their infinite diversity. And also remember: somebody out there is listening.

7. Usage

All this talk about good words and bad words brings us to a gray but important area called "usage." What is good usage? What is good English? What newly minted words is it O.K. to use, and who is to be the judge? Is it O.K. to use "O.K."?

Earlier I mentioned an incident of college students hassling the administration, and in the last chapter I described myself as a word freak. Here are two typical specimens that have crept into the language in the past five years. "Hassle" is both a verb and a noun, meaning to give somebody a hard time, or the act of being given a hard time, and anyone who has ever been hassled by a petty bureaucrat for not properly filling out Form 35-BT will agree that it sounds exactly right. "Freak" in this new usage means an enthusiast, and there is no missing the aura of obsession that goes with calling somebody a jazz freak, or a chess freak, or a sun freak, though it would probably be pushing my luck to describe a man who compulsively visits circus sideshows as a freak freak.

Anyway, I accept both of these new arrivals wholeheartedly. I don't consider them slang, or put quotation marks around them to show that I'm mucking about in the argot of the counter-culture and really know better. They're good words and we need them to express what they express. But I still won't accept "notables" and "greats" and "upcoming" and countless other new-comers. They are cheap words and we *don't* need them.

Why is one word good and another word cheap? I can't give you an answer because usage has no fixed boundaries or rules. Language is a fabric that changes from one week to another, adding new strands and dropping old ones, and even word freaks fight over what is allowable, often reaching their decision on a wholly subjective basis such as taste ("notables" is sleazy). Which still leaves the question of who our tastemakers are.

The question was confronted by the editors of a brand-new dictionary, *The American Heritage Dictionary*, at the outset of their task in the mid-1960's. They assembled a "Panel on Usage" to help them appraise the new words and dubious constructions that had come knocking at the door. Which should be ushered in, which thrown out on their ear? The panel consisted of 104 men and women—mostly writers, poets, editors and teachers—who were known for caring about the language and trying to use it well.

I was a member of the panel, and over the next few years I kept getting questionnaires. Would I accept "finalize" and "esca-late"? How did I feel about "It's me"? Would I allow "like" to be used as a conjunction—like so many people do? How about "mighty," as in "mighty fine"?

We were told that in the dictionary our opinions would be tabulated in a separate "Usage Note" so that readers could tell how we voted. The questionnaire also left room for any comments that we might feel impelled to make—a chance that the panelists seized avidly, as we found when the dictionary was published and our comments were released to the press. Not surprisingly, our passions ran high.

"Good God, no! Never!" cried Barbara W. Tuchman, asked about the verb "to author." Scholarship hath no fury like that of a language purist faced with sludge, and I share Mrs. Tuch-man's vow that "author" should never be authorized, just as I agree with Lewis Mumford that the adverb "good" should be "left as the exclusive property of Ernest Hemingway" and with Gerald Carson that "normalcy" should be "permitted only to admirers of the late Warren G. Harding."

But guardians of usage are only doing half their job if they merely keep the language from becoming sloppy. Any oaf can rule that the suffix "wise," as in "mediawise," is oafwise, or that being "rather unique" is no more possible than being rather pregnant. The other half of the job is to help the language grow by welcoming any immigrant that will bring strength or color.

Therefore I was glad to see that 97 percent of us voted to admit "dropout," which is clean and vivid, but that only 47 percent would accept "senior citizen," which is pretentious and patronizing, typical of the pudgy new intruders from the land of sociology, where a janitor is a maintenance engineer. I'm glad we accepted "escalate," the kind of verbal contraption which I generally dislike but which the Vietnam war gave a precise meaning, complete with overtones of blunder.

I'm glad we took into full membership all sorts of robust words that previous dictionaries had derided as "colloquial": adjectives like "rambunctious," verbs like "stall" and "trigger" and "rile," nouns like "shambles" and "tycoon" and "trek," the latter approved by 78 percent to mean any difficult trip, as in "the commuter's daily trek to Manhattan." Originally it was a Cape Dutch word applied to the Boers' arduous journey by ox wagon. But our panel evidently felt that the Manhattan commuter's daily trek is no less arduous.

Still, 22 percent of us were unwilling to let "trek" slip into general usage. This was the virtue of revealing how our panel voted— it put our agreements and our discords on display, and now a writer who is in doubt can conduct himself accordingly. Thus our 95 percent vote against "myself," as in "He invited Mary and myself to dinner," a word condemned as "prissy," horrible" and "a genteelism," ought to warn off anyone who doesn't want to be prissy, horrible and genteel. As Red Smith put it, " 'Myself' is the refuge of idiots taught early that 'me' is a dirty word."

On the other hand, only 66 percent rejected the verb "to

contact," and only half opposed the split infinitive and the verbs "to fault" and "to bus." So only 50 percent of your readers will fault you if you decide to voluntarily call your school board and to bus your children to another town. If you contact your school board you risk your reputation by another 16 percent. Our apparent rule of thumb was stated by Theodore M. Bernstein: "We should apply the test of convenience. Does the word fill a real need? If it does, let's give it a franchise." I agree with Bernstein. "Hassle," for instance, seems to me to fill a real need.

All of this merely confirms what lexicographers have always known: that the laws of usage are relative, bending with the taste of the lawmaker. One of our panelists, Katherine Anne Porter, called "O.K." a "detestable vulgarity" and claimed that she has never spoken the word in her life, whereas I freely admit that I have spoken the word "O.K." "Most," as in "most everyone," was scorned as "cute farmer talk" by Isaac Asimov and embraced as a "good English idiom" by Virgil Thomson.

"Regime," meaning any administration, as in "the Truman regime," drew the approval of most everyone on the panel, as did "dynasty." But they drew the wrath of Jacques Barzun, who said, "These are technical terms, you blasted non-historians!" Probably I gave my O.K. to "regime" when I filled out the questionnaire. Now, chided by Barzun for imprecision, I think it looks like journalese. One of the words that *I* railed against was "personality," as in a "TV personality." But now I wonder if it isn't the only word for that vast swarm of people who are famous for being famous—and, possibly, for nothing else. What, for instance, do the Gabor sisters really *do*?

In the end it comes down to one question: What is "correct" usage? We have no king to establish the King's English; we only have the President's English—which we don't want. Webster, long a defender of the faith, muddied the waters in 1961 with its permissive Third Edition, which argued that almost anything goes as long as somebody uses it, noting that "ain't" is "used orally in most parts of the U.S. by many cultivated speakers."

Just where Webster cultivated those speakers I ain't sure.

Nevertheless it's true that the spoken language is always looser than the written language, and *The American Heritage Dictionary* properly put its question to us in both forms. Often we allowed an oral idiom which we forbade in print as too informal, fully realizing, however, that "the pen must at length comply with the tongue," as Samuel Johnson said, and that today's spoken garbage may be tomorrow's written gold. Usewise it gradually becomes O.K. Certainly the growing acceptance of the split infinitive, or of the preposition at the end of a sentence, proves that formal syntax can't hold the fort forever against a speaker's more comfortable way of getting the same thing said, and as for "It's me," who would defend to the death "It is I"? Only a purity freak.

Our panel recognized that correctness can even vary within a particular word. We voted heavily against "cohort," for instance, as a synonym for "colleague," except where the tone was jocular. Thus a professor would not be among his cohorts at a faculty meeting, but they would abound at his college reunion, wearing funny hats. We rejected "too" as a synonym for "very," as in "His health is not too good." Whose health is? But we approved it in wry or humorous use, as in "He was not too happy when she ignored him."

These may seem like picayune distinctions. They're not. They are signals to the reader that you are sensitive to the many shadings of usage. "Too," when substituted for "very," is clutter—"he didn't feel too much like going shopping"—and should be cut out. But the wry example in the previous paragraph is worthy of Ring Lardner. It adds a tinge of sarcasm that wouldn't otherwise be there.

Did any pattern emerge from the opinions of our panel when we finally ended our task, or were we just flexing our prejudices and pedantries? Luckily, a pattern did emerge, and it offers a useful guideline. In general we turned out to be liberal in accepting new words and phrases, but conservative in grammar. It would be foolish, for instance, to reject a word as perfect as "dropout," or to pretend that countless words are not entering the gates of correct usage every day, borne on the winds of science and technology, fad and fashion, social change and social concern: "moonscape," "printout," "unisex," "dashiki," "pantyhose," "sky-jacker," "consumerism," "wetlands," "biodegradable," "sexist," "lib," "machismo," "uptight," "paraprofessional" and hundreds more.

It would also be foolish not to at least consider all the wonderfully short words invented by the counterculture as a way of lashing back at the bloated verbiage of the Establishment: "bag," "scene," "trip," "rap," "crash," "trash," "fuzz," "funky," "split," "rip-off," "downer," "bummer," et al. If brevity is a prize, these are sure winners.

The only trouble with accepting words that entered the language overnight is that they have a tendency to leave as abruptly as they came. The "happenings" of the late 1960's no longer happen, "out of sight" is out of sight, nobody does his "thing" anymore, "relevant" has been hooted out of the room, and where only yesterday we wanted our leaders to have "charisma," today we want a man who has "clout." We also want him to be "together." Be vigilant, therefore, about instant change. The writer who cares about usage must always know the quick from the dead.

As for the area where our usage panel was conservative, we strictly upheld most of the classic distinctions in grammar— "can" and "may," "fewer" and "less," "eldest" and "oldest," etc.— and decried the classic errors, insisting that "flout" still doesn't mean "flaunt," no matter how many writers flaunt their ignorance by flouting the rule, and that "fortuitous" still means "accidental," "disinterested" still means "impartial," and "infer" doesn't mean "imply."

Here we were motivated by our love of the language's beautiful precision. We hate to see our favorite tools mistreated. As Dwight Macdonald put it, "Simple illiteracy is no basis for linguistic evolution." This is where correct usage will win or lose you the

readers you would most like to win. Know the difference between
a "reference" and an "allusion," between "connive" and "conspire,"
between "compare with" and "compare to." If you must use
"comprise," use it right.

"I choose always the grammatical form unless it sounds af-
fected," explained Marianne Moore, and that finally is where our
usage panel took its stand. We were not pedants, so hung up on
correctness that we didn't want the language to keep refreshing
itself with phrases like "hung up." But that didn't mean that we
had to accept every atrocity that has come stumbling in, like
"hopefully."

Prayerfully this chapter will help you to approach the question
of "What is good usage?" but fearfully you will sometimes slide
off the track. And if that sentence doesn't explain why "hopefully" is bad usage, go back to "Go." Do not collect $200.

PART II

8. Unity

You learn to write by writing. It is a truism worn thin by repetition, but it is still true, and it can't be repeated often enough. The only way to learn to write is to force yourself to produce a certain number of words on a regular basis.

If you went to work for a newspaper which required you to write two or three articles every day, you would be a better writer after six months. You wouldn't necessarily be writing well —your style might still be pedestrian, full of clutter and clichés. But at least you would be exercising your powers of putting the English language on paper, gaining confidence, and identifying the commonest problems.

All writing is ultimately a question of solving a problem. It may be a problem of where to obtain the facts, or how to organize the material. It may be a problem of approach or attitude, tone or style. Whatever it is, it has to be confronted and solved.

Sometimes you will despair of finding the right solution—or any solution. You will think: "If I live to be ninety I'll never get out of this mess I'm in." I have often thought it myself. But when I finally do solve the problem it's because I have written millions and millions of words. Like a surgeon doing his five hundredth appendix operation, I've been there before and have a surer instinct than the beginner about how to fix what has gone wrong.

So now I'll put you to actual writing. First I wanted to give you a set of attitudes and broader principles. I wanted you to realize how easily the reader can get lost. I wanted to point out that the American language is becoming more bloated every week with pompous locutions and paralyzing jargon, all highly contagious. I wanted to give you a respect for your tools—words —and to emphasize that some are better than others. Above all, I wanted you to strive for freshness.

Now the task is to apply these principles to the various forms that nonfiction can take: the interview, the travel piece, the science article, sports, criticism, humor and all the hybrid species that can result from mixing them together. Every form has its special pitfalls. But all of them share one horrible problem: how to get started. No element of writing causes so much anguish as "the lead," and with almost no further ado I will try to wrestle it into partial submission. The only ado that I will first commit is to suggest that before you struggle with the lead you make certain decisions about what tone you want to adopt. Get your unities straight.

Unity is the anchor of good writing. It not only keeps the reader from straggling off in all directions; it satisfies his subconscious need for order and assures him that all is well at the helm. Therefore choose from among the many variables and stick to your choice.

One choice is unity of pronoun. Are you going to write in the first person as a participant or in the third person as an observer? Or even in the second person, that darling of sportswriters hung up on Hemingway ("You knew this had to be the most spine-tingling clash of giants you'd ever seen from a pressbox seat, and you weren't just some green kid who was still wet behind the ears")?

Unity of tense is another choice. Most people write mainly in the past tense ("I went up to Boston the other day"), but some people write agreeably in the present ("I'm sitting in the dining car of the Yankee Limited and we're pulling into Boston"). What is not agreeable is to switch back and forth. I'm not saying that you can't use more than one tense. Obviously the whole purpose of tenses is to enable a writer to deal with time in its various gradations from the past to the hypothetical future ("When I telephoned my girl from the Boston station I realized that if I had written to tell her I would be coming she would have waited for me"). What I am saying is that you must choose the tense in which you are *principally* going to address the reader, no matter how many glances you may take backward or forward along the way.

Another choice is unity of mood. You might want to talk to the reader in the casual and chatty voice that *The New Yorker* has so strenuously refined. Or you might want to approach him with a certain formality to describe a serious event or to acquaint him with a set of important facts. Both tones are acceptable; in fact, *any* tone is acceptable. But don't mix two or three.

Such fatal mixtures are common in the nonfiction of writers who haven't yet learned control. Travel writing is a conspicuous case. "My wife Ann and I had always wanted to visit Hong Kong," the writer begins, his blood astir with reminiscence, "and one day last spring we found ourselves looking at an airline poster and I said, 'Let's go!' The kids were grown up or in school," he continues, and proceeds to describe in genial detail how they stopped off in Hawaii and had such a comical time changing their money at the Hong Kong airport and finding their hotel. Fine. He is a real person taking us along on a real trip, and we can identify with him and Ann.

Suddenly he turns into a travel brochure. "Hong Kong affords many fascinating experiences to the curious sightseer," he writes. "One can ride the picturesque ferry from Kowloon and gawk at the myriad sampans as they scuttle across the teeming harbor, or take a day's trip to browse in the alleys of fabled Macao with its colorful history as a den of smuggling and intrigue. You will want to take the quaint funicular that climbs . . ." Then we get back to him and Ann and their efforts to eat at Chinese restaurants, and again all is well. Everyone is interested in food and we are being told about a personal quest.

Then suddenly the writer is a guidebook: "To enter Hong Kong it is necessary to have a valid passport but no visa is required. You should definitely be immunized against smallpox and you would also be well advised to consult your physician with regard to a possible inoculation for typhoid. The climate in Hong Kong is seasonable except in July and August when . . ." Our writer is gone, and so is Ann, and so—very soon—are we.

It is not that the scuttling sampans and the smallpox shots should not be included. What annoys us is that the writer never decided what kind of article he wanted to write or how he wanted to approach us. He comes at us in many guises, depending on what kind of material he is trying to purvey. Instead of controlling his material, his material is controlling him. This wouldn't happen if he took time to establish certain unities.

Therefore ask yourself some basic questions before you start. For example: "In what capacity am I going to address the reader?" (Reporter? Provider of information? Average man?) "What pronoun and tense am I going to use?" "What style?" (Impersonal reportorial? Personal but formal? Personal and casual?) "What attitude am I going to take toward the material?" (Involved? Detached? Judgmental? Ironic? Amused?) "How much do I want to cover?" "What one point do I really want to make?"

The last two questions are more important than they might seem. Most nonfiction writers have a definitiveness complex. They feel that their article must be the last word and the most comprehensive word. It's a commendable impulse, but there is no definitive article. What you think is definitive today will turn undefinitive by tomorrow, and the writer who doggedly pursues every last fact will find himself pursuing the rainbow and never settling down to write. Decide what corner of your subject you are going to bite off, and be content to cover it well and stop. You can always come back another day and bite off another corner.

As for what point you want to make, I'll state as a useful rule of thumb that every successful piece of nonfiction should leave the reader with one provocative thought that he didn't have before. Not two thoughts, or five—just one. So try to decide what point you most want to leave in the reader's mind. It will not only give you a better idea of what route you ought to follow and what destination you hope to reach; it will also affect your decision about tone and attitude. Some points are best made by dry understatement, some by heavy irony.

Once you have these unities decided, there is no material that you can't work into your frame. If the man writing about Hong Kong had chosen to write solely in the conversational vein about what he and Ann thought and did, he would have found a natural way to weave into his narrative whatever he wanted to tell us about the Kowloon ferry and the local weather. His personality and purpose would be intact, and his article would hold together.

Now it's possible that you will make these prior decisions and then discover that they were not the right ones. The material seems to be leading you in an unexpected direction where you are more comfortable writing in a different tone. This is not abnormal—the very act of writing will often summon out of the brain some cluster of thoughts or memories which you didn't anticipate.

Don't fight such a current if it feels right. Trust your material if it is taking you into terrain that you didn't intend to enter but where the vibrations are good. Adjust your style and your mood accordingly and proceed to whatever destination you reach. Don't ever become the prisoner of a preconceived plan. Writing is no respecter of blueprints—it is too subjective a process, too full of surprises.

Of course if this happens, the second part of your article will be badly out of joint with the first. But at least you will know which part is truest to your instincts. Then it is just a matter of making repairs. Go back to the beginning and rewrite it so that the mood and style are consistent.

There is nothing in such a method to be ashamed of. Scissors and paste are honorable writers' tools. Just remember that all the unities must be fitted into the edifice that you finally put together, however backwardly they may fall into place, or it will soon come tumbling down.

9. The Lead

The most important sentence in any article is the first one. If it doesn't induce the reader to proceed to the second sentence, your article is dead. And if the second sentence doesn't induce him to continue to the third sentence, it is equally dead. Of such a progression of sentences, each tugging the reader forward until he is safely hooked, a writer constructs that fateful unit: the "lead."

How long should the lead be? One or two paragraphs? Four or five? There is no pat answer. Some leads hook the reader with just a few well-baited sentences; others amble on for several pages, exerting a slow but steady pull. Every article poses a different problem, and the only valid test is: Does it work? Your lead may not be the best of all possible leads, but if it does the job that it is supposed to do, be thankful and proceed.

Sometimes the length may depend on the audience that you are writing for. Readers of *The New Yorker* or of a literary review, for instance, expect the writer to start somewhat discursively, and they will stick with him for the pleasure of wondering where he will emerge as he moves in leisurely circles toward his eventual point. But I urge you not to count on the reader to stick around. He is a fidgety fellow who wants to know—very soon—what's in it for him.

Therefore the lead must capture the reader immediately and force him to keep reading. It must cajole him with freshness or novelty or paradox, or with humor, or with surprise, or with an unusual idea, or an interesting fact, or a question. Anything will do as long as it nudges his curiosity and tugs at his sleeve.

Next the lead must do some real work. It must provide a few hard details that tell the reader why the piece was written and why he ought to read it. But don't dwell on the reason. Coax the reader a little more; keep him inquisitive.

Continue to build. Every paragraph should amplify the one that preceded it. Give more thought to adding solid detail and less to entertaining the reader. But take special care with the last sentence of each paragraph—it is the crucial springboard to the next paragraph. Try to give that sentence an extra twist of humor or surprise, like the periodic "snapper" in the routine of a stand-up comic. Make the reader smile and you've got him for at least one paragraph more.

Let's look at a few leads that vary in pace but are alike in maintaining pressure. I'll start with three columns of my own that first appeared in, respectively, *Life, The Saturday Evening Post* and *Look*—three magazines which, judging by the comments of readers, found their consumers mainly in barbershops, hairdressing salons and airplanes ("I was getting a haircut the other day and I saw your article"). I mention this as a reminder that far more periodical reading is done in America under the dryer than under the reading lamp, so there isn't much time for the writer to fool around.

I don't claim that these are three best leads I could have found; I only know that they work. The first is the lead of a piece called "Block That Chickenfurter":

I've often wondered what goes into a hot dog. Now I know and I wish I didn't.

Two very short sentences. But it would be hard not to continue to the second paragraph:

My trouble began when the Department of Agriculture published the hot dog's ingredients—everything that may legally qualify—because it was asked by the poultry industry to relax the conditions under which the ingredients might also include chicken. In other words, can a chickenfurter find happiness in the land of the frank?

One sentence that explains the incident on which the column is based. Then a snapper to restore the easygoing tone.

Judging by the 1,066 mainly hostile answers that the Department got when it sent out a questionnaire on this point, the very thought is unthinkable. The public mood was most felicitously caught by the woman who replied: "I don't eat feather meat of no kind."

Another fact and another smile. Whenever you are lucky enough to meet a quotation as funny as that, find a way to use it—preferably at the end of a paragraph.

The article then specifies what the Department of Agriculture says may go into a hot dog—a list that includes "the edible part of the muscle of cattle, sheep, swine or goats, in the diaphragm, in the heart or in the esophagus . . . [but not including] the muscle found in the lips, snout or ears."

From there it progresses—not without an involuntary reflex around the esophagus—into an account of the controversy between the poultry interests and the frankfurter interests, which in turn leads to the point that Americans will eat anything that even remotely resembles a hot dog. Implicit at the end is the larger point that Americans don't know, or care, what goes into the food they eat. The style of the article has remained casual and touched with humor throughout. But its content turns out to be more serious than the reader expected when he was drawn into it by a somewhat whimsical lead.

Here's another lead, from an article that was called "Does He or Doesn't He?":

Until this year I have always wanted to smell as good as the next man. But now the next man wants to smell too good. The boom in male cosmetics is sweeping America at such speed—sales went over half a billion dollars in 1965 alone and are growing fast—that one of the country's most popular entertainers recently refused to tell the name of the scent that he was wearing. Too many other men, he explained, would also start to wear it.

That entertainer's secret would be safe with me. He could tell me the name of his scent tomorrow and I swear I wouldn't call up my pharmacy. Nor do I own a single face cream, and I've never been to any of the men's "hair stylists" for a tinting or a spray. I go to a funny old-fashioned barber who just cuts my hair and doesn't try to make me look younger than when I went in. If anything, his conversation sends me out older.

The last sentence does no real work—it's a tiny joke and not a very good one. But it propels the reader on to the third paragraph, where the article gets down to business:

All of this makes me a member of America's newest minority group: an adult male untouched by rejuvenating lotions, fragrances and dyes. "A case of galloping vanity has hit men in this country," Eugenia Sheppard writes, "and any minute now there'll be masks, moisturizers, home hair coloring and hair sprays for men."

That minute is almost here. Hardly a day goes by when I don't read in the paper or see in a TV commercial some new evidence that . . .

The article goes on to document the growing American belief that a man who looks young and glossy is more competent than his visibly aging colleague. From there it veers off, in a turn just sharp enough to catch the reader off balance, to arrive at the sober point which it intended all along to reach—that this is a crazy way for a society to operate. In style the unities continue to be intact: "I don't want to touch—or retouch—a hair of the gray heads that ponder my financial, legal and medical affairs. . . . I like to think that every one of their gray hairs was honorably earned, every facial line etched by a mistake that they will not make again." But the substance is far deeper than the reader anticipated when he was being pampered through the first few paragraphs. What remains with him is not the lead, but the point.

A slightly slower lead, luring the reader more with curiosity than with humor, introduced a piece called "Thank God for Nuts":

> By any reasonable standard, nobody would want to look twice—or even once—at the piece of slippery elm bark from Clear Lake, Wisc., birthplace of pitcher Burleigh Grimes, that is on display at the National Baseball Museum and Hall of Fame in Cooperstown, N.Y. As the label explains, it is the kind of bark that Grimes chewed during games "to increase saliva for throwing the spitball. When wet, the ball sailed to the plate in deceptive fashion." This would seem to be one of the least interesting facts available in America today.
>
> But baseball fans can't be judged by any reasonable standard. We are obsessed by the minutiae of the game and nagged for the rest of our lives by the memory of players we once saw play. No item is therefore too trivial which puts us back in touch with them. I am just old enough to remember Burleigh Grimes and his well-moistened pitches sailing deceptively to the plate, and when I found his bark I studied it as intently as if I had come upon the Rosetta Stone. "So *that's* how he did it," I thought, peering at the odd botanical relic. "Slippery elm! I'll be damned."
>
> This was only one of several hundred encounters that I had with my own boyhood as I prowled through the Museum, a handsome brick building on Main Street, only a peanut bag's throw from the pasture where Abner Doubleday allegedly invented the game in 1839. Probably no other museum is so personal a pilgrimage to our past . . .

The reader is now safely hooked, and the hardest part of the writer's job is over.

One reason for citing this lead is to point out that salvation often lies not in the writer's style but in some odd fact that he was able to unearth. I remember that I went up to Cooperstown and spent a whole afternoon in the museum, taking voluminous notes. Jostled everywhere by nostalgia, I gazed with reverence at Lou Gehrig's locker and Bobby Thomson's game-winning bat; I sat in a grandstand seat brought from the Polo Grounds, dug my unspiked soles into the home plate from Ebbets Field, and dutifully copied all the labels and captions that might be useful.

"These are the shoes that touched home plate as Ted finished his journey around the bases," said the label identifying the shoes worn by Ted Williams when he hit a home run on his last time at bat. The shoes were in much better shape than the pair—rotted open at the sides—that belonged to Walter Johnson. But again the caption provided exactly the kind of justifying fact that a baseball nut would want. "My feet must be comfortable when I'm out there a-pitching," the great Walter said.

The museum closed at five and I returned to my motel secure in my memories and in my research. But instinct told me to go back the next morning for a final tour, and it was only then that I noticed Burleigh Grimes' slippery elm bark, which struck me as an ideal lead. It still does.

One moral of this story is that you should always collect more material than you will eventually use. Every article is strong in proportion to the surplus of details from which you can choose the few that will serve you best—if you don't go on gathering facts forever. At some point you must decide to stop researching and start writing.

An even more important moral is to look for your material everywhere, not just by reading the obvious sources and interviewing the obvious people. Look at signs and at billboards and at all the junk written along the American roadside. Read the labels on our packages and the instructions on our toys, the claims on our medicines and the graffiti on our walls.

Read the fillers, so rich in self-esteem, that come spilling out of your monthly statement from the electric company and the telephone company and the bank. Read menus and catalogues and second-class mail. Nose about in obscure crannies of the newspaper, like the Sunday real estate section—you can tell the temper of a society by what patio accessories it wants. Our daily landscape is thick with absurd messages and portents. Notice them. They not only have a certain social significance; they are often just quirky enough to make a lead that is different from everybody else's.

And speaking of everybody else's lead, there are several categories that I'd be glad never to see again. One is the future archeologist: "When some future archeologist stumbles upon the remains of our civilization a thousand years from now, what will he make of the jukebox?" I'm tired of him already and he's not even here. I'm also tired of the visitor from Mars: "If a creature from Mars landed on our planet tomorrow, he would be amazed to see hordes of scantily clad earthlings lying on the sand and barbecuing their skins." And I'm tired of the cute event that just happened to happen "one day not long ago" or on a conveniently recent Saturday afternoon. "One day not long ago a small button-nosed boy was walking with his dog, Terry, in a field outside Paramus, N.J., when he saw something that looked strangely like a balloon rising out of the ground." Let's retire the future archeologist and the man from Mars and the button-nosed boy. Try to give your lead a freshness of perception or detail.

Consider this lead, by Joan Didion, on a piece called "7000 Romaine, Los Angeles 38":

Seven Thousand Romaine Street is in that part of Los Angeles familiar to admirers of Raymond Chandler and Dashiell Hammett: the underside of Hollywood, south of Sunset Boulevard, a middle-class slum of "model studios" and warehouses and two-family bungalows. Because Paramount and Columbia and Desilu and the Samuel Goldwyn studios are nearby, many of the people who live around here have some tenuous connection with the motion-picture in-

dustry. They once processed fan photographs, say, or knew
Jean Harlow's manicurist. 7000 Romaine looks itself like a
faded movie exterior, a pastel building with chipped *art
moderne* detailing, the windows now either boarded or paned
with chicken-wire glass and, at the entrance, among the
dusty oleander, a rubber mat that reads WELCOME.
Actually no one is welcome, for 7000 Romaine belongs to
Howard Hughes, and the door is locked. That the Hughes
"communications center" should lie here in the dull sunlight
of Hammett-Chandler country is one of those circumstances
that satisfy one's suspicion that life is indeed a scenario, for
the Hughes empire has been in our time the only industrial
complex in the world—involving, over the years, machinery
manufacture, foreign oil-tool subsidiaries, a brewery, two
airlines, immense real-estate holdings, a major motion-
picture studio, and an electronics and missile operation—
run by a man whose *modus operandi* most closely resembles
that of a character in *The Big Sleep.*
       As it happens, I live not far from 7000 Romaine, and I
make a point of driving past it every now and then, I suppose
in the same spirit that Arthurian scholars visit the Cornish
coast. I am interested in the folklore of Howard Hughes . . .

What is pulling us into this article—toward, we hope, some
glimpse of how Hughes operates, some hint of the riddle of the
Sphinx—is the steady accretion of facts that have pathos and
faded glamour. Knowing Jean Harlow's manicurist is such a
minimal link to glory, the unwelcoming welcome mat such a
queer relic of a golden age when Hollywood's windows weren't
paned with chicken-wire glass and the roost was ruled by giants
like Mayer and DeMille and Zanuck who could actually be seen
alive and exercising their mighty power. We want to know more;
we read on.
       Another writer whose leads I admire is Garry Wills. Almost
every chapter in his *Nixon Agonistes,* which originated as a series
of magazine articles, begins with an arrangement of sentences

that dazzle me with their gathering momentum and mordant truth:

FEBRUARY, 1968: It is early morning in Wisconsin, in Appleton, air heavy with the rot of wood pulp. This is the place where Joe McCarthy lived and was buried—a place, once, for Nixon to seek out on campaign; then, for a longer time, a place to steer shy of. He has outlived both times, partially. And it is too late to care in any event: the entire American topography is either graveyard, for him, or minefield—ground he must walk delicately, revenant amid the tombstones, whistling in histrionic unconcern.

Monday evening, on plan, Nixon's jet turned and returned through the gauzy late Miami afternoon. The trick was not to touch the runway too early—while the 6:30 TV shows were opening with their résumé stories on the first day of the convention. And not to land too late—when the slanting light would be grayed for the color cameras. The team had chosen 6:38 as optimum time for live coverage; so the plane circled a half hour, responsive to the intricate countdown, signaling the networks, holding, easing into its pattern, landing, sidling, disgorging staff, and—6:38—epiphany out of a pink sky.

Spiro Agnew's career has about it a somnambulistic sure-footedness, an inevitability of advance, that reminds one of Mencken's Coolidge, of the juggernaut of snooze. In an election-eve TV broadcast, Hubert Humphrey proudly displayed Ed Muskie, his monkish second-string Eugene McCarthy. Nixon, on the same night, sat alone, remasticating answers for Bud Wilkinson, his kept TV interrogator. No Agnew in sight. It was said that Nixon regretted his choice, his deal with Thurmond. But Agnew was a guided missile, swung into place, aimed, activated, launched with the minute calculation that marks Nixon. Once the missile was fired, the less attention it drew to itself the better—like a torpedo churning quiet toward its goal. Agnew has a neckless, lidded flow to him, with wraparound hair, a tubular perfection to his suits or golf outfits, quiet burbling oratory. Subaquatic. He was almost out of sight by campaign's end; but a good sonar system could hear him burrowing ahead, on course.

Three typically fine leads, all doing their job with precise detail, unexpected imagery and words as surprising as a rare bird. Wills is holding his reader in a tight grip but never patronizing him. And yet there can be no fixed rules. Within the broad principle of not letting the reader get away, every writer must approach his subject in a manner that most naturally suits what he is writing about and who he is. In proof of which, I'll close with the lead of an article on rugby written by Richard Burton, the actor. Its second sentence is one of the longest I've ever seen, but it is under control all the way. Besides, it sounds very Welsh, and if that's how Welshmen talk it's how they ought to write:

It's difficult for me to know where to start with rugby. I come from a fanatically rugby-conscious Welsh miner's family, know so much about it, have read so much about it, have heard with delight so many massive lies and stupendous exaggerations about it and have contributed my own fair share, and five of my six brothers played it, one with some distinction, and I mean I even knew a Welsh woman from Taibach who before a home match at Aberavon would drop goals from around 40 yards with either foot to entertain the crowd, and her name, I remember, was Annie Mort and she wore sturdy shoes, the kind one reads about in books as "sensible," though the recipient of a kick from one of Annie's shoes would have been not so much sensible as insensible, and I even knew a chap called Five-Cush Cannon who won the sixth replay of a cup final (the previous five encounters having ended with the scores 0-0, 0-0, 0-0, 0-0, 0-0, including extra time) by throwing the ball over the bar from a scrum 10 yards out in a deep fog and claiming a dropped goal. And getting it.

10. The Ending

After so many words suggesting how to get started, I should add a few on how to stop. Knowing when to end an article is far more important than most writers realize. In fact, you should give as much thought to choosing your last sentence as you did to your first. Well, almost as much.

This may seem ridiculous. If the reader has stuck with you from the beginning, trailing you around blind corners and over bumpy terrain, surely he won't leave when the end is in sight. But he will—because the end that is in sight often turns out to be a mirage. Like the minister's sermon that builds to a series of perfect conclusions which never conclude, an article that doesn't stop at its proper stopping place is suddenly a drag and therefore, ultimately, a failure.

We are most of us still prisoners of the lesson pounded into us by the composition teachers of our youth: that every story must have a beginning, a middle and an end. We can still visualize the outline, with its Roman numerals (I, II and III), which staked out the road that we would faithfully trudge, and its sub-numerals (IIa and IIb) denoting lesser paths down which we would briefly poke. But we always promised to get back to III and summarize our journey.

This is all right for elementary and high school students uncertain of their ground. It forces them to see that every piece of writing should have a logical design which introduces and develops a theme. It's a lesson worth knowing at any age—even the professional writer is adrift more often than he would like to admit. But if you are going to write good nonfiction, you must wriggle out of III's dread grip.

You will know you have arrived at III when you see emerging from your typewriter a sentence that begins, "In sum, therefore, it can be noted that . . ." Or a question that asks, "What insights, then, have we been able to glean from . . . ?" These are signals to the reader that you are about to repeat in compressed form what you have already told him in detail. His interest begins to falter; the tension that you have built begins to sag.

Yet you will be true to Miss Potter, your teacher, who made you swear eternal fealty to the holy outline. You remind the reader of what can, in sum, therefore, be noted. You go gleaning one more time in insights that you have already adduced.

But the reader hears the laborious sound of cranking. He sees what you are doing and how bored you are by it. He feels the stirrings of resentment. Why didn't you give more thought to how you were going to wind this thing up? Or are you summarizing because you think he was too dumb to get the point? Still, you keep cranking. But the reader has another option. He quits.

This is the negative reason for realizing the importance of the last sentence. Failure to know where that sentence should occur —and what it should consist of—can wreck an article which until its final stage has been tightly constructed.

The positive reason for ending well is not just to avoid ending badly, but because a good last sentence—or paragraph—is a joy in itself. It has its own virtues which give the reader a lift and which linger when the article is over.

The perfect ending should take the reader slightly by surprise and yet seem exactly right to him. He didn't expect the article to end so soon, or so abruptly, or to say what it said. But he knows it when he sees it. Like a good lead, it works. It is like the

curtain line in a theatrical comedy. We are in the middle of a
scene (we think) when suddenly one of the actors says something
funny, or outrageous, or epigrammatic, and the lights go out.
We are momentarily startled to find the scene over, and then
delighted by the aptness of how it ended. What delights us,
subconsciously, is the playwright's perfect control.

For the nonfiction writer, the simplest way of putting this into
a rule is: when you're ready to stop, stop. If you have presented
all the facts and made the point that you want to make, look for
the nearest exit.

Often it takes just a few sentences to get out of the article in
the same style that you used to get in. Going back to Garry
Wills' *Nixon Agonistes*, here is how he ends a visit to Nixon's
home town of Whittier:

> Even one day in Whittier, spent imagining the America
> of Nixon's childhood, is suffocating. That world has a locker-
> room smell, of spiritual athleticism. As I drove back toward
> Los Angeles that night, along Whittier Boulevard, wide lane
> enscrolled on either side with continuous neon scallops, the
> sulphur of Los Angeles seemed a better thing to breathe
> than the muggy air, heavy with moral perspiring, of Whittier.

There is no need to retrace the steps already taken. "Moral per-
spiring" says it all.

Or see how Wills ends the chapter on Agnew, whom we last
saw launched missile-like, subaquatic, into the political ocean
of American life:

> There is a difference between ambition and opportunism.
> Leisurely "Ted" is not driven by Nixon's demons. He does
> not knock himself out; he does not even do his homework.
> But he is opportunistic—not cynically so; when lucky breaks
> come, one takes them, grateful. Man's function is to reap
> the fruits of our beneficent system. How foolish of "the
> kids" not to understand this. As he told them in the cam-
> paign: "You may give us your symptoms; we will make the

diagnosis and we, the Establishment, will implement the cure." It is a message that he did not try to make to Miami's blacks.

The blunt irony of that final sentence brings echoes of Mencken rumbling down the decades again, as so often happens for me when one of America's bleakest truths is seen through a glass plainly. Here is how Mencken ends his appraisal of Coolidge, whose appeal to the "customers" was that his "government governed hardly at all; thus the ideal of Jefferson was realized at last, and the Jeffersonians were delighted":

> We suffer most, not when the White House is a peaceful dormitory, but when it [has] a tin-pot Paul bawling from the roof. Counting out Harding as a cipher only, Dr. Coolidge was preceded by one World Saver and followed by two more. What enlightened American, having to choose between any of them and another Coolidge, would hesitate for an instant? There were no thrills while he reigned, but neither were there any headaches. He had no ideas, and he was not a nuisance.

These are the elements to look for when instinct tells you that it's time to stop. Both the Agnew sentence and the Coolidge sentence send the reader on his way quickly and with a provocative thought to take along. The notion of Coolidge having no ideas and not being a nuisance is bound to leave a residue of enjoyment. It works.

But what often works best is a quotation. Try to find in your notes some remark which has a sense of finality, or which is funny, or which adds an unexpected last detail. Sometimes it will jump out at you in the process of writing. Put it aside and save it. If the remark doesn't jump out, go back and look for it among all the things said or written by anyone mentioned in the article.

Ten years ago, when Woody Allen was just becoming established as the nation's resident neurotic, I wrote the first long magazine piece that took note of his arrival. It ended like this:

"If people come away relating to me as a person," Allen
says, "rather than just enjoying my jokes; if they come away
wanting to hear me again, no matter what I might talk
about, then I'm succeeding." Judging by the returns, he is.
Woody Allen is Mr. Related-To, Mr. Pop Therapy, of the
mid-1960's, and he seems a good bet to hold the franchise for
many years.

Yet he does have a problem all his own, unshared by, un-
related to, the rest of America. "I'm obsessed," he says, "by
the fact that my mother genuinely resembles Groucho Marx."

There's a remark from so far out in left field that nobody could
see it coming. The surprise that it carries is tremendous. How
could it not be a perfect ending?

Another person I interviewed was Guy Lombardo. The annual
shepherding in of the New Year by Lombardo to the strains of
"Auld Lang Syne" is so deeply embedded in our folklore that
anyone might assume that Americans have sung this song at
midnight on December 31 since the days of the early Scottish
settlers. But as I found when I wrote an article on Lombardo's
umbilical tie to New Year's Eve, the fact is more unusual than
the assumption, and the logical place to put it was at the end:

> Lombardo doesn't remember that first New Year's Eve
> [in 1929] as anything special, but it was not long before he
> took personal custody of the event, holding it by the feat of
> "being on consistently," as he points out, "from the early days
> of radio right through the era of television." Rival band-
> leaders never had a chance, for Lombardo was sponsored
> by both major networks. NBC had the half-hour before
> midnight, and on this program the Royal Canadians would
> cheat the old year of one minute and play "Auld Lang Syne"
> at 11:59. Then CBS would take over at 12 and Lombardo
> would play it again. Thus the nation had two official mid-
> nights but never knew it.
>
> But the main reason why Lombardo became identified

as the Ghost of New Years Past, Present and To Come, he says, "is because 'Auld Lang Syne' is our theme song—and was long before anyone ever heard us on the radio. In our part of western Ontario, where there's a large Scottish population, it was traditional for bands to end every dance with 'Auld Lang Syne.' We didn't think it was known here. When we left Canada we had no idea we'd ever play it again."

I won't flout the advice sprinkled through this chapter by summarizing why these two quotations make good endings. Allen and Lombardo, reaching into their own emotions and memories, do more than a writer possibly could. I will merely point out that surprise is one of the most refreshing commodities in nonfiction and that, as I'll try to demonstrate next, there is nothing like human detail to make a story come alive.

11. The Interview

Get people talking. Learn to ask questions that will elicit answers about what is most interesting or vivid in their lives. Nothing so animates writing as someone telling what he thinks or what he does—in his own words.

His own words will always be better than your words, even if you are the most elegant stylist in the land. They carry the inflection of his speaking voice and the idiosyncrasies of how he puts a sentence together. They contain the regionalisms of his conversation and the lingo of his trade. They convey his enthusiasms. This is a person talking to the reader directly, not through the filter of a writer. As soon as a writer steps in, everybody else's experience becomes secondhand.

Therefore learn how to conduct an interview. Whatever form of nonfiction you write, it will come alive in proportion to the number of "quotes" that you can weave into it naturally as you go along. Often, in fact, you will find yourself embarking on an article so apparently lifeless—the history of an institution, perhaps, or some local issue such as storm sewers—that you will quail at the prospect of keeping your readers, or even yourself, awake.

Take heart. You will find the solution if you look for the human element. Somewhere in every drab institution are men and women who have a fierce attachment to what they are doing and are rich repositories of lore. Somewhere behind every storm sewer is a politician whose future hangs on getting it installed and a widow who has always lived on the block and is outraged that some damn-fool legislator thinks it will wash away. Find these people to tell your story and it won't be drab.

I have proved this to myself many times. In 1961 I undertook to write a small book for The New York Public Library to celebrate the fiftieth anniversary of its main building on Fifth Avenue. On the surface it seemed to be just the story of a marble building and millions of musty volumes. But behind the façade I found that the Library had nineteen research divisions, each with a curator supervising a hoard of treasures and oddities, from Washington's handwritten Farewell Address to 750,000 movie stills. I decided to interview all these curators to learn what was in their collections, what they were adding to keep up with new areas of knowledge, and how their rooms were being used.

I found, for instance, that the Science and Technology division had a collection of patents second only to that of the United States Patent Office and was therefore almost a second home to the city's patent lawyers. But it also had a daily stream of men and women who obviously thought they were on the verge of discovering perpetual motion. "Everybody's got something to invent," the curator explained, "but they won't tell us what they're looking for—maybe because they think we'll patent it ourselves."

The whole building turned out to be just such a mixture of scholars and searchers and crackpots, and my story, though ostensibly the chronicle of an institution, was really a story about people.

I used the same approach in a long article about Sotheby's, the thriving London auction firm. Sotheby's was also divided into various domains, such as silver and porcelain and art, each with an expert in charge, and, like the Library, it subsisted on the whims of a capricious public. The experts were like department heads in a small college, and all of them had anecdotes that were unique both in substance and in the manner of telling:

"We just sit here like Micawber waiting for things to come in," said R. S. Timewell, head of the furniture department. "Recently an old lady near Cambridge wrote that she wanted to raise two thousand pounds and asked if I would go through her house and see if her furniture would fetch that much. I did, and there was absolutely nothing of value. As I was about to leave I said, 'Have I seen *everything*?' She said I had, except for a maid's room that she hadn't bothered to show me. The room had a very fine 18th-century chest that the old lady was using to store blankets in. 'Your worries are over,' I told her, 'if you sell that chest.' She said, 'But that's quite impossible—where will I store my blankets?'"

My worries were over, too. By listening to the quizzical scholars who ran the business and to the men and women who flocked there every morning bearing unloved objects found in British attics ("I'm afraid it *isn't* Queen Anne, Madam—much nearer Queen Victoria, unfortunately") I got as much human detail as a writer could want.

Finally, when I was asked to write a history of the Book-of-the-Month Club to mark its fortieth birthday and 200-millionth book, I thought I would encounter nothing but inert matter. But again I found a peppery human element on both sides of the fence, for the books have always been selected by a panel of strong-minded judges and sent to equally stubborn subscribers, who never hesitated to wrap up a book that they didn't like and to send it right back.

I was given more than 1,000 pages of transcribed interviews with the five original judges (Heywood Broun, Henry Seidel Canby, Dorothy Canfield, Christopher Morley and William Allen White), to which I added my own interviews with the Club's founder, Harry Scherman, and with the judges who were then active (John Mason Brown, Clifton Fadiman, Gilbert Highet and John K. Hutchens). The result was four decades' worth of personal memories on how America's reading tastes had changed, and why, and even the books took on a life of their own and became characters in my story:

"Probably it's difficult for anyone who remembers the prodigious success of 'Gone With the Wind,'" Dorothy Canfield said, "to think how it would have seemed to people who encountered it simply as a very, very long and detailed book about the Civil War and its aftermath. We had never heard of the author and didn't have anybody else's opinion on it. It was chosen with a little difficulty, because some of the characterization was not very authentic or convincing. But as a narrative it had the quality which the French call *attention*: it made you want to turn over the page to see what happens next. I remember that someone commented, 'Well, people may not like it very much, but nobody can deny that it gives a lot of reading for your money.' Its tremendous success was, I must say, about as surprising to us as to anybody else."

These three examples are typical of the kind of information that is locked inside people's heads which a good nonfiction writer must unlock. The best way to practice is to go out and interview people. The interview itself is one of the most common and popular nonfiction forms, so you might as well master it early.

How should you start? First, decide what person you want to interview. If you are a college student, don't interview your roommate. With all due respect for what a fine fellow he is, he probably doesn't have much to say that the rest of us want to hear. To learn the craft of nonfiction you must push yourself out into the real world—your town or your city or your county— and pretend that you are writing for a real publication. If it helps, decide which publication you are hypothetically writing for. In any case, choose as your subject someone whose job is so important, or interesting, or unusual that the average reader would want to read about him.

This doesn't mean that he has to be president of General Motors. He can be the owner of the local pizza parlor or supermarket or hairdressing academy. He can be the fisherman who puts out every morning, or the Little League manager, or the cop. He can be the butcher, the baker or—better yet, if you can find him—the candlestick maker. Look for the women in your community who are beginning to unravel the old myths about what the two sexes were foreordained to do. Choose, in short, someone who touches some corner of the reader's life.

Interviewing is one of those skills that you can only get better at. You will never again feel so ill at ease as when you try it for the first time, and probably you will never feel entirely comfortable prodding another person for answers that he or she may be too shy to reveal, or too inarticulate. But at least half of the skill is purely mechanical. The rest is instinct—knowing how to make the other person relax, when to push, when to listen, when to stop. And this can all be learned with experience.

The basic tools for an interview are paper and two or three well-sharpened pencils. Is that the most insultingly obvious advice you have ever been given? You'd be surprised how many writers venture forth to stalk their quarry with no pencil, or with one that breaks, or with a pen that doesn't work, and with nothing to write on. "Be prepared" is as apt a motto for the nonfiction writer on his mundane rounds as it is for the Boy Scout alert for the traditional old lady trying to cross the street.

But keep your notebook or paper out of sight until you need it. There is nothing less likely to relax a person than the arrival of someone with a stenographer's pad. You both need time to get to know each other. Small talk at this point is a big asset. Take a while just to chat, gauging what sort of person you are dealing with, getting him to trust you.

Never go into an interview without doing whatever homework you can. If you are interviewing a town official, know his voting record. If it's an actor, know what plays he has been in. You will be resented if you inquire about facts that you could have learned in advance.

Make a list of likely questions—it will save you the vast embarrassment of going dry in mid-interview. Perhaps you won't need it; better questions will occur to you, or the person being interviewed will veer off at an angle that you couldn't have foreseen. Here you can only go by intuition. If he strays hopelessly off the subject, drag him back. If you like the new direction that he is taking, follow him and forget the questions that you intended to ask.

Many beginning interviewers are crippled by the fear that they are imposing on the other person and have no right to invade his privacy. This fear is almost 100 percent unfounded. Unless the other person is Howard Hughes he is delighted that somebody wants to interview him. Most men lead lives, if not of quiet desperation, at least of desperate quietness, and they jump at a chance to talk about their work to an outsider who seems eager to listen.

This doesn't necessarily mean that it will go well. In general you will be talking to people who have never been interviewed before, and they will warm to the process awkwardly, self-consciously, perhaps not giving you anything that you can use. Come back another day; it will go better. You will both even begin to enjoy it—proof that you aren't forcing your victim to do something that he doesn't really want to do.

Speaking of tools, you will ask if it's all right to use a tape recorder. Why not just take one along, start it going, and forget all that business of pencil and paper?

Obviously the tape recorder is a superb instrument for capturing what people have to say—especially people who, for reasons of their culture or education or temperament, would never get around to writing it down. I admire the books of Studs Terkel, like *Hard Times: The Story of the Great Depression*, which he "wrote" by recording long interviews with ordinary people and stitching the results into coherent shape. I admire the oral histories of Spanish-speaking people similarly "written" by Oscar Lewis, such as *La Vida*. In this realm of social anthropology the tape recorder is literally invaluable. I also like the question-and-answer interviews, obtained by tape recorder, that have long been published in *Playboy* and *Rolling Stone* and are now turning up in other magazines. They have the sound of spontaneity and the refreshing absence of a writer hovering over the product and burnishing it to a high gloss.

But, strictly, this isn't writing. It's a process of asking questions and then pruning and splicing the answers, and I can testify that it takes an infinitude of time and care and labor. People who seem to be talking into the tape recorder with linear precision and taut economy turn out, when the interview is transcribed, to have been stumbling so aimlessly over the sands of grammar that they have hardly completed a single decent sentence. Hence my admiration for Terkel and Lewis and other stewards of the spoken word. The seemingly simple use of a tape recorder isn't simple.

But my main reasons for warning you off it are practical and tangible. The practical hazards hardly need to be mentioned. One is that you don't usually have a tape recorder with you—you are more apt to have a pencil. Another is that tape recorders malfunction. Few moments in journalism are as glum as the return of a reporter with "a really great story," followed by his pushing of the PLAY button and total silence.

My tangible reason is that there should be a relationship between a writer and his materials, just as there should be a relationship between an artist and his canvas and his brush. The act of taking notes is, however fragmentary, an act of writing. To bypass this process by having someone talk into a machine is to lose the subtle mystery of seeing words emerge as you put them on paper.

This is especially important in an interview. Someone is telling you something; you are writing it down. It is a human transaction that has been going on for thousands of years.

But there is a problem: he is talking faster than you can write. You are still scribbling Sentence A when he zooms into Sentence B. You drop Sentence A and pursue him into Sentence B, meanwhile trying to hold the rest of Sentence A in your inner ear and hoping that Sentence C will be a dud that you can skip altogether, using the time to catch up. Unfortunately, you now have your man going at high speed. He is at last saying all the things that you have been trying to cajole out of him for an hour, and saying them with what seems to be Churchillian eloquence. Your inner ear is clogging up with sentences that you want to grab before they slip away.

Tell him to stop. Just say, "Hold it a minute, please," and write until you catch up. It's a request that you should never hesitate to make. What you are trying to do with your feverish scribbling, after all, is to quote him correctly, and nobody wants to be misquoted.

With practice you will write faster and develop some form of shorthand. You will find yourself devising abbreviations for often-used words and also omitting the small connective syntax. As soon as the interview is over, fill in all the missing words that you can remember. Complete the uncompleted sentences. Most of them will still be lingering just within the bounds of recall.

When you get home, type out your notes—now an almost illegible scrawl—so that you can read them easily. This not only makes the interview accessible, along with any clippings or other materials that you may have assembled. It enables you to review in tranquillity a torrent of words that you wrote in haste, and thereby discover what the person really said.

You will find that he said much that is redundant or dull. Try to single out the quotations that are most important or colorful. You will be tempted to use all the words that are in your notes because you performed the laborious chore of getting all the words down. This is no reason for putting the reader to the same trouble. Your job is to distill the essence.

What about your obligation to the person you interviewed? To what extent can you cut or juggle his words? This question vexes every writer returning from his first interview—and it should. But the answer is not hard if you keep in mind two standards: brevity and fair play.

Your ethical duty to the person being interviewed is to present his position accurately. If he carefully weighed two sides of an issue and you only quote his views of one side, making him seem to favor that position, you will misrepresent what he told you. Or you might misrepresent him by quoting him out of context, or by choosing only some flashy remark without adding the serious afterthought. Your first obligation is to the person who gave you the interview and to his version of the story. You are dealing with a man's honor and reputation—and also with your own.

But after that your duty is to the reader. He deserves the smallest package. Most people meander in their conversation, filling it with irrelevant tales and trivia. Much of it is delightful, but it is still trivia. Your interview will be strong to the extent that you get the main points made without waste.

Therefore if you find on page 5 of your notes a comment which perfectly amplifies a point on page 2—a point made earlier in the interview—you will do everyone a favor if you link the two thoughts, letting the second sentence follow and illustrate the first. This may violate the truth of how the interview progressed, but you will be true to the intent of what was said. Play with the "quotes" by all means—selecting, rejecting, thinning, transposing their order, saving a good one for the end. Just make sure that the play is fair. Don't change any words or let the cutting of a sentence distort the proper context of what remains.

This is really my case against the tape recorder. A writer should always be able to *see* his materials. If your interview is on tape you become a listener, forever fussing with the machine, running it backward to find a brilliant remark that you can't quite find, running it forward, stopping, starting, driving yourself crazy. Be a writer. Write things down.

As for how to organize the interview, every one is different, so I will leave you to discern its logical shape and will only add a few technical hints.

The lead obviously should tell the reader, like all leads, why the person is worth reading about. What is his claim to our time and attention?

Thereafter, try to achieve a balance between what the subject is saying in *his* words and what you are writing in *your* words to explain and to connect. If you quote a person for three or four consecutive paragraphs, this becomes monotonous. Quotations are livelier when you break them up, making periodic appearances in your role as guide. You are still the writer—don't relinquish control. But make your appearances useful; don't just insert one of those dreary sentences which shout to the reader that your sole purpose is to break up a string of quotations ("He stopped and tapped his pipe on a nearby ashtray and I noticed that his fingers were quite long").

When you use a quotation, start the sentence with it. Don't lead up to it with a vapid phrase saying what the man said.

> GOOD: "I usually like to go downtown once a week," Mr. Smith said, "and have lunch with some of my old friends."
> BAD: Mr. Smith said that he liked to "go downtown once a week and have lunch with some of my old friends."

The first sentence has vitality, the second is dead. In fact, nothing is deader than to start a sentence with a "Mr. Smith said" construction—it's where countless readers stop reading. If the man said it, let him say it and get the sentence off to a warm, human start.

But be careful where you break the quotation. Do it as soon as you naturally can, so that the reader knows who is talking, but not where it will destroy the rhythm or the sense. Notice how the following three variants all inflict some kind of damage:

> "I usually like," Mr. Smith said, "to go downtown once a week and have lunch with some of my old friends."
> "I usually like to go downtown," Mr. Smith said, "once a week and have lunch with some of my old friends."
> "I usually like to go downtown once a week and have lunch," Mr. Smith said, "with some of my old friends."

Finally, don't strain to find synonyms for "he said." Don't make your man assert, aver and expostulate just to avoid re-

peating "he said," and please—please!—don't write "he smiled"
or "he grinned." I have never heard anybody smile. The reader's
eye skips over "he said" anyway, so it's not worth a lot of fuss.
If you crave variety, choose synonyms that catch the shifting
nature of the conversation. "He pointed out," "he explained," "he
replied," "he added"—these all carry a particular meaning. But
don't use "he added" if the man is merely averring and not
putting a postscript on what he just said.

I'll close by adding as a postscript a passage from *The Bottom of
the Harbor*, by Joseph Mitchell, my own favorite writer of long
nonfiction articles and possibly America's best. The book consists of various articles that Mitchell wrote for *The New Yorker*
about people who live and work around the waterfront. One
reason I admire Joseph Mitchell is that he is a master of the un-
commonly difficult art of writing about the so-called common
man without ever patronizing him.

This is part of an interview with the captain of a fishing boat
called a "dragger" that operates out of Stonington, Connecticut.
Note the deceptively simple style, the exactness of detail, and
especially the deft interweaving of Mitchell's words with those
of the captain, Ellery Thompson:

> Ellery is a self-taught B-flat trumpet player. While living
> on the *Eleanor*, he spent many evenings in the cabin by him-
> self practicing hymns and patriotic music. Sometimes, out on
> the grounds, if he had a few minutes to kill, he would go
> below and practice. One afternoon, blundering around the
> Hell Hole in a thick summer fog, he grew tired of cranking
> the foghorn and got out his trumpet and stood on deck and
> played "The Star-Spangled Banner" over and over, alarming
> the crews of other draggers fogbound in the area, who
> thought an excursion boat was bearing down on them. After
> he went back to sleeping at home, he continued to practice
> in the evenings, but he had to give it up before long because
> of its effect on his mother's health.

"At that time," he says, "I was working hard on three hymns—'Up From the Grave He Arose,' 'There Is a Fountain Filled With Blood' and 'What a Friend We Have in Jesus.' I had 'What a Friend' just about where I wanted it. One evening after supper, I went in the parlor as usual and Ma was sitting on the settee reading the *Ladies' Home Journal* and I took the easy chair and went to work on 'What a Friend.' I was running through it the second or third time when, all of a sudden, Ma bust out crying. I laid my trumpet down and I asked her what in the world was the matter. 'That trumpet's what's the matter,' Ma said. 'It makes me sad.' She said it made her so sad she was having nightmares and losing weight. Under the circumstances, I decided whatever trumpet practice I did in the future, I would do it four or five miles out at sea."

Ellery walks with a pronounced stoop, favoring his left shoulder, where the rheumatism has settled, and he takes his time. "If I start to hustle and bustle," he says, "everything I eat repeats and repeats." He abhors hurry; he thinks that humanity in general has got ahead of itself. He once threatened to fire a man in his crew because he worked too hard. . . .

Ellery is about as self-sufficient as a man can be. He has no wife, no politics and no religion. "I put off getting married until I got me a good big boat," he says. "When I got the boat and got it paid for, the Depression struck. There's mighty few women that'll eat fish three times a day, and that's about all I had to offer. I kept putting it off until times got better. When times got better, I got the rheumatism. And a man in his middle forties with the chronic rheumatism, there's not much of the old Romeo left in him."

Ellery is a member of only one organization. "I'm a Mason," he says. "Aside from that, the only thing I belong to is the human race." His father was a Republican and his mother is a Democrat; he says he has never put any dependence in either party and has never once voted for any-

body. His family belongs to the Baptist Church; he says he
has somehow managed to get along without it. "I enjoy
hymns," he says. "I enjoy the old ones, the gloomy ones.
I used to go to church just to hear the good old hymns, but
the sermons finally drove me away."

12. Travel

Next to knowing how to write about people, you should know how to write about a place. People and places are the twin pillars on which most nonfiction is built. Every human event happens somewhere, and the reader wants to know what that "somewhere" was like.

In a few cases you will need only a paragraph or two to sketch the setting of an event. But more often you will need to evoke the mood of a whole neighborhood or town to give texture to the story you are telling. And in certain cases, such as the travel piece itself—that perennial form in which you recount how you lived on a houseboat in Kashmir or crossed the Sahara by bus—descriptive detail will be the main substance.

Whatever the proportion, it would seem to be relatively easy. The dismal truth is that it is very hard. It must be hard because it is in this area that most writers—professional and amateur— produce not only their worst work, but work that is just plain terrible.

The terrible work has nothing to do with some terrible flaw of character. On the contrary, it results from the virtue of enthusiasm. Nobody turns so quickly into a bore as a traveler home from his travels. He enjoyed his trip so much that he wants to tell us all about it—and "all" is what we don't want to hear. We only want to hear some. What made his trip different from everybody else's? What can he tell us that we don't already know? We don't want him to describe every ride at Disneyland, or tell us that the Grand Canyon is awesome, or that Venice has canals. If one of the rides at Disneyland got stuck, or if somebody fell into the awesome Grand Canyon, *that* would be worth hearing about.

It is natural for all of us when we have gone to a certain place to feel that somehow we are the first people who ever went there or thought such sensitive thoughts about it. Fair enough—it is what keeps us going and validates our experience. Who can visit the Tower of London without musing on the wives of Henry VIII, or visit Egypt and not be moved by the size and antiquity of the pyramids?

But this is ground already covered by many people. As a writer you must keep a tight rein on your subjective self—the traveler touched by new sights and sounds and smells—and keep an objective eye on the reader. The article that records what you did every day on your trip will fascinate you because it was your trip. Will it fascinate the reader? Nine times out of ten it won't. The mere agglomeration of detail is no free pass to his interest. The detail must in some way be significant.

The other big trap is style. Nowhere else in nonfiction do writers use such syrupy words and groaning platitudes. Adjectives that you would squirm to use in conversation—"roseate," "wondrous," "fabled"—are common currency. Half the sights seen in a day's sightseeing are "quaint," especially windmills and covered bridges. They are certified for quaintness.

It is a style of soft words which under hard examination mean nothing, or which mean different things to different people: "attractive," "charming," "romantic." To write that "the city has its own attractiveness" is no help—every city does. And who will define "charm," except possibly the owner of a charm school? Or "romantic"? These are subjective concepts in the eye of the beholder. One man's romantic sunrise is another man's hangover.

Travelese is a land "where old meets new." I'm amazed at the number of places where old meets new. Old never meets old. The meeting occurs in the "twisting alleys" and "bustling thoroughfares" of storied Tangier or picturesque Zanzibar. This is terrain dotted with "byways," usually half-forgotten or at least hidden. It is a world where inanimate objects spring to transitive life: storefronts smile, buildings boast, ruins beckon and the very chimney tops sing their immemorial song of welcome. The clichés bloom with very fertility.

How can you overcome such fearful odds and write well about a place? My advice can be reduced to two principles—one of style, the other of substance.

First, choose your words with unusual care. If a phrase comes to you easily, look at it with deep suspicion—it's probably one of the innumerable clichés which have woven their way so tightly into the fabric of travel writing that it takes a special effort *not* to use them. Also resist straining for the luminous lyrical phrase to describe the wondrous waterfall. At best it will make you sound artificial—unlike yourself—and at worst pompous. Strive for fresh words and images. Leave "myriad" and their ilk to the poets. Leave "ilk" to anyone who will take it away.

As for substance, be intensely selective. If you are describing a beach, don't write that "the shore was scattered with rocks" or that "occasionally a seagull flew over." Shores have a tendency to be scattered with rocks and to be flown over by seagulls. Eliminate every such fact that is a known attribute: don't tell us that the sea had waves and that the sand was white. Find details that are significant. They may be important to your narrative. They may be unusual, or colorful, or comic, or entertaining. But make sure they are details that do useful work.

I'll give you some examples from various writers, widely different in temperament but alike in the effectiveness of the detail that they chose. The first is from an article by Joan Didion called "Some Dreamers of the Golden Dream." It is about a lurid crime that occurred in the San Bernardino Valley of California, and in this early passage the writer is taking us, as if in her own car, away from urban civilization to the lonely stretch of road where Lucille Miller's Volkswagen so unaccountably caught fire:

This is the California where it is easy to Dial-A-Devotion, but hard to buy a book. This is the country of the teased hair and the Capris and the girls for whom all life's promise comes down to a waltz-length white wedding dress and the birth of a Kimberly or a Sherry or a Debbi and a Tijuana divorce and a return to hairdressers' school. "We were just crazy kids," they say without regret, and look to the future. The future always looks good in the golden land, because no one remembers the past. Here is where the hot wind blows and the old ways do not seem relevant, where the divorce rate is double the national average and where one person in every 38 lives in a trailer. Here is the last stop for all those who come from somewhere else, for all those who drifted away from the cold and the past and the old ways. Here is where they are trying to find a new life style, trying to find it in the only places they know to look: the movies and the newspapers. The case of Lucille Marie Maxwell Miller is a tabloid monument to the new style.

Imagine Banyan Street first, because Banyan is where it happened. The way to Banyan is to drive west from San Bernardino out Foothill Boulevard, Route 66: past the Santa Fe switching yards, the Forty Winks Motel. Past the motel that is 19 stucco tepees: "SLEEP IN A WIGWAM—GET MORE FOR YOUR WAMPUM." Past Fontana Drag City and Fontana Church of the Nazarene and the Pit Stop A Go-Go; past Kaiser Steel, through Cucamonga, out to the Kapu Kai Restaurant-Bar and Coffee Shop, at the corner of Route 66 and Carnelian Avenue. Up Carnelian Avenue from the Kapu Kai, which means "Forbidden Seas," the sub-division flags whip in the harsh wind. "HALF-ACRE RANCHES! SNACK BARS! TRAVERTINE ENTRIES! $95

DOWN." It is the trail of an intention gone haywire, the flotsam of the New California. But after a while the signs thin out on Carnelian Avenue, and the houses are no longer the bright pastels of the Springtime Home owners but the faded bungalows of the people who grow a few grapes and keep a few chickens out here, and then the hill gets steeper and the road climbs and even the bungalows are few, and here—desolate, roughly surfaced, lined with eucalyptus and lemon groves—is Banyan Street.

In only two paragraphs we have a feeling not only for the tackiness of the New California landscape, with its stucco tepees and instant housing and borrowed Hawaiian romance, but for the pathetic impermanence of the lives and pretensions of the people who have alighted there. All the details—statistics and names and signs—are doing helpful work.

Another kind of "travel" writing, the personal memoir, a rich form because it taps so many wells of childhood and growing up, also depends on the writer's ability to call back what made his neighborhood distinctive, his early life unique. One of my favorite examples is Alfred Kazin's *A Walker in the City.* The locale is Brownsville, a Jewish ghetto in Brooklyn, and the detail tends to be sensual. Smells, for instance, are evocative for Kazin. For another writer, what stirs a specific memory might be a sound, or the theme song of an old radio show.

Here is a fragment of Kazin's youth:

It was the darkness and emptiness of the streets I liked most about Friday evening, as if in preparation for that day of rest and worship which the Jews greet "as a bride"—that day when the very touch of money is prohibited, all work, all travel, all household duties, even to the turning on and off of a light—Jewry had found its way past its tormented heart to some ancient still center of itself. I waited for the streets to go dark on Friday evening as other children waited for the Christmas lights. . . . When I returned home after three, the warm odor of a coffee cake baking in the oven, and the sight of my mother on her hands and knees scrubbing the linoleum on the dining room floor filled me with such tenderness that I could feel my senses reaching out to embrace every single object in our household.

My great moment came at six, when my father returned from work, his overalls smelling faintly of turpentine and shellac, white drops of silver paint still gleaming on his chin. Hanging his overcoat in the long dark hall that led into our kitchen, he would leave in one pocket a loosely folded copy of the New York *World*; and then everything that beckoned to me from that other hemisphere of my brain beyond the East River would start up from the smell of fresh newsprint and the sight of the globe on the front page. It was a paper that carried special associations for me with Brooklyn Bridge. They published the *World* under the green dome of Park Row overlooking the bridge; the fresh salt air of New York harbor lingered for me in the smell of paint and damp newsprint in the hall. I felt that my father brought the outside straight into our house with each day's copy.

Another area where your success will rest on freshness of detail is the vast field of exploration and adventure, especially when it also involves the history of an obscure region and the reconstruction of events that happened long ago. For me the best hand at this difficult work is Alan Moorehead. I have followed him across much of Africa and Australia and Asia and the Pacific, always struck with admiration bordering on disbelief that he could collate such a wealth of present and past experience and write about it with seemingly effortless warmth.

His books, *The White Nile* and *The Blue Nile*, are marvels of craftsmanship. Though they deal with a huge gallery of men and women who sought the source of those rivers in the nineteenth century, bedeviled by hostile nature and hostile tribes, illness and ignorance, jurisdictional squabbles in the interior and back home in England, all the characters are wonderfully alive, and so is

Moorehead as a writer, stitching his own observations of Africa together with what he has extracted from the journals of the explorers who preceded him up the Nile long ago.

Moorehead's style is so uniformly pleasant that I could quote from almost any page of his books or articles. The following excerpt is as good as any because it is descriptive material of the kind that is ordinarily so susceptible to banalities and purple prose:

At least seventeen years have gone by since I first flew up the valley of the upper Nile, starting the journey at Khartoum, in the Sudan, and ending it nearly two thousand miles away, at the source of the river, in Uganda. I was a war correspondent at the time, on my way from one campaign, in the western desert of Egypt, to another, in Ethiopia. Even then, when planes did not fly nearly so high as they do today, there was not very much to be seen from the air except the endless desert and the meandering green line of the river, but there were frequent stops along the way, and these I remember just as distinctly as one remembers the islands on a long ocean voyage.

Before we started, we were held up for three or four days at Khartoum with engine trouble. It was April, the hottest time of the year—so hot, in fact, that it was slightly painful just to touch the porcelain sides of your bathtub when you got up in the morning. A fearsome sandstorm known as a *haboob* was blowing, and it was only at the very end of the long, torpid day that the town woke up at last. Each evening, about an hour before the light began to fail, I used to walk down to the zoo with a book. The Khartoum Zoo is quite unlike any other zoo in the world. It lies on the left bank of the Blue Nile, just upstream from the point where the White Nile comes in from southern Sudan, and it covers hardly more than two or three acres.

The animals and the birds do not have that vacant and dispirited air that seems to overtake tropical creatures when they are transported to cold climates in the north. They have all been born here in this hothouse atmosphere, and many of them are not kept in cages; they simply roam about in their natural state, grazing on the grass and the bushes or wading in the pond. At the hour when I used to go to the zoo, there were hardly any visitors, and as I sat there reading, the zebras, the antelopes and many kinds of long-legged birds would gather around in a quiet and hesitating way that was something between curiosity and fear. It was very pleasant and very peaceful, and this made it all the more surprising one evening when I looked up from my book and found General de Gaulle standing before me. He was wearing a pale-blue kepi and a tropical uniform, and as I rose from my bench he saluted in a friendly, informal way and went off to see the giraffes. Heaven knows what he was doing in that outlandish place. I saw him only twice more during the war—once at Casablanca, with Roosevelt and Churchill, and then during the Liberation of Paris, when he marched down the Champs-Elysées at the head of his men and we were all in tears.

Finally, let me come to that troublesome organism, the travel piece itself. This is the article whose primary purpose is to describe a certain place—never mind such collateral purposes as telling a story or reconstructing a set of events. Practice writing this kind of article, and just because I call it a travel piece I don't mean that you have to go to Khartoum. Go to your local shopping mall, or bowling alley, or park. Or write about your vacation. But whatever place you write about, go there long enough or often enough to isolate the qualities that make it special. Usually this will be some combination of the place and the people who inhabit it. If it's your local bowling alley it will be a mixture of the atmosphere inside and the regular patrons. If it's a foreign city it will be some mixture of the ancient culture and its present populace. Try to find it.

A master of this feat of detection is the English author V. S.

Pritchett, one of the best and most versatile of nonfiction writers. Consider what he squeezes out of a visit to Istanbul:

> Istanbul has meant so much to the imagination that the reality shocks most travelers. We cannot get the sultans out of our minds. We half expect to find them still cross-legged and jewelled on their divans. We remember tales of the harem. The truth is that Istanbul has no glory except its situation. It is a city of steep, cobbled, noisy hills. . . .
>
> Mostly the shops sell cloth, clothes, stockings, shoes, the Greek traders rushing out, with cloth unrolled, at any potential customer, the Turks passively waiting. Porters shout; everyone shouts; you are butted by horses, knocked sideways by loads of bedding, and, through all this, you see one of the miraculous sights of Turkey—a demure youth carrying a brass tray suspended on three chains, and in the exact center of the tray a small glass of red tea. He never spills it; he maneuvers it through chaos to his boss, who is sitting on the doorstep of his shop.
>
> One realizes there are two breeds in Turkey: those who carry and those who sit. No one sits quite so relaxedly, expertly, beatifically as a Turk; he sits with every inch of his body; his very face sits. He sits as if he inherited the art from generations of sultans in the palace above Seraglio Point. Nothing he likes better than to invite you to sit with him in his shop or in his office with half a dozen other sitters: a few polite inquiries about your age, your marriage, the sex of your children, the number of your relations, and where and how you live, and then, like the other sitters, you clear your throat with a hawk that surpasses anything heard in Lisbon, New York or Sheffield, and join the general silence.

I like the phrase "his very face sits"—just four short words, but they convey an idea so fanciful that they take us by surprise. They also tell us a great deal about Turks. I'll never be able to visit Turkey again without noticing its sitters. With one quick

insight Pritchett has caught a whole national trait. This is the
essence of good writing about a place. Distill the important from
the immaterial.

I'm reminded by Pritchett's own nationality that the English
have long excelled at a distinctive form of travel writing that I
should mention before traveling on—the article that is less notable
for what the writer extracts from a place than for what the place
extracts from him. New sights touch off thoughts that would
otherwise never have entered his mind. If travel is broadening,
it should broaden more than just our knowledge of, say, how a
Gothic cathedral looks or how the French make wine. It should
generate a whole constellation of new ideas about how men and
women work and play, raise their children, worship their gods,
live and die. Certainly the books written by Britain's "desert
eccentrics"—scholar-adventurers like Charles Doughty and T. E.
Lawrence who chose to live among the Arabs—derive much
of their strange power from the reflections born of surviving in
so harsh and minimal an environment.

So when you write about a place, try to draw the best out of it.
But if the process should work in reverse, let it draw the best out
of you. In this sense, probably the finest travel book written
by an American is *Walden*, though Thoreau only went a few
miles out of town, and today a growing number of nonfiction
writers are finding their voice by hitting the road, going back to
the land or pondering the mysteries of nature.

No writer has been more creatively provoked by the search
for modern America than Norman Mailer. Shrewd and witty
insights about our latest values fly like sparks out of his books—
typically, his book about the launching of Apollo 11, *Of a Fire on
the Moon*, and about the faceless new breed of men who reared
it and raised it into space. What did it all mean? Was the achieve-
ment stirring or sterile? Even Mailer isn't sure at the end, and
Mailer is seldom at a loss for certitudes. But there has been much
to think about along the way.

Let me leave you with him, then, on the eve of the launch,

staring with "some portion of a million" rubberneckers across the water to the spaceship that would lift itself off its pad in the morning and take three men to the moon:

> In the distance she glowed for all the world like some white stone Madonna in the mountains, welcoming footsore travelers at dusk. Perhaps it was an unforeseen game of the lighting, but America had not had its movie premieres for nothing, nor its Rockettes in Radio City and 50 million squares tooling the tourist miles over the years to Big Town to buy a ticket to spectacle and back home again. If you were going to have a Hollywood premiere and arc lights, a million out to watch and a spaceship which looked across the evening flutter like the light on the Shrine of Our Lady outside any church in Brooklyn or Bay Ridge, then by God you might just as well have this spectacle on the premiere trip to the moon. That deserved a searchlight or two!

There were new industries in America these years. After five decades of suspense movies, and movies of the Wild West, after the adventures of several generations of men in two world wars and Korea and Vietnam, after 16 years of "Playboy" and American iconization of the gravity-defying breast and the sun-ripened buttock, after ten years of the greatest professional football, after a hundred years and more of a tradition that the frontier was open and would never close, and after 20 more perplexing technological years when prosperity came to nearly every White pocket, and technology put out its plastic, its superhighways, its supermarkets, its appliances, its suburbs, its smog, and its intimation that the frontier was damn shut, shut like a boulder on a rabbit burrow, America had erupted from this pressure between its love of adventure and its fear that adventure was completely shut down; America had spewed out on the road. The country had become a nation of campers, of cars toting trailers, of cars pulling tent-trailers, of truck-campers, top-of-car tent packs, Volkswagen buses converted to ambula-

tory bedrooms, jeeps with Chic Sale houses built on the back,
Land-Rovers with bunks, Broncos with more bunks—any
way a man could get out of the house with his buddies or his
family or his grandmother, and take to the road and find
some ten by twenty feet of grass not posted, not tenanted,
and not too muddy, he would camp. All over America in the
summer the night fields were now filled with Americans
sleeping on air mattresses which reposed on plastic cloth
floors of plastic cloth tents—what a sweet smell of Corporate
Chemical, what a vat and void to mix with all the balmy
fermy chlorophylls and pollens of nature! America the Sani-
tary, and America the Wild, went out to sleep in the woods,
Sanitary-Lobe and Wild-Lobe nesting neatly together,
schizophrenic twins in the skull case of the good family
American.

13. Bits & Pieces

This is a chapter of scraps and morsels—small admonitions on many points which I have collected under one, as they say, umbrella.

VERBS. Use active verbs unless there is no comfortable way to get around using a passive verb. The difference between an active-verb style and a passive-verb style—in pace, clarity and vigor—is the difference between life and death for a writer.

"Joe hit him" is strong. "He was hit by Joe" is weak. The first is short and vivid and direct; it leaves no doubt about who did what. The second is necessarily longer and it has an insipid quality; something was done by somebody to someone else. A style which consists mainly of passive constructions, especially if the sentences are long, saps the reader's energy. He is never quite certain of what is being perpetrated by whom and on whom.

I use "perpetrated" because it's the kind of word that passive-voice writers are fond of. They prefer long words of Latin origin to short Anglo-Saxon words—which compounds their trouble and makes their sentences still more glutinous. Short is generally better than long, and don't go Latin if the Anglo-Saxons have given you a word that conveys the same idea.

Verbs are the most important of all your tools. They push the sentence forward and give it momentum. Active verbs push hard; passive verbs tug fitfully. Most verbs also carry somewhere in their imagery or in their sound a suggestion of what they mean: flail, poke, dazzle, squash, beguile, pamper, swagger, wheedle, vex. I would bet that no other language has such a vast supply of verbs so bright with color. Don't choose one that is dull or merely serviceable. Make active verbs activate your sentences, and try to avoid the kind that need an appended preposition or two to complete their work. Don't "set up" a business that you can establish. Don't "come upon" an object that you can discover, or "take hold of" one that you can grab. Don't "put up with" pain; bear it.

Cultivate this rich crop. And if you want to see how active verbs give vitality and flair to the written word, don't just go back go Hemingway or Thurber or Thoreau. I commend to you the King James Bible, William Shakespeare and Abraham Lincoln.

ADVERBS. Most adverbs are unnecessary. You will clutter your sentence and annoy the reader if you choose a verb that has a precise meaning and then add an adverb that carries the same meaning. Don't tell us that the radio blared loudly— "blare" connotes loudness. Don't write that someone clenched his teeth tightly—there is no other way to clench teeth. Again and again in careless writing, self-sufficient verbs are weakened by redundant adverbs.

So are countless adjectives and other parts of speech: "Totally flabbergasted," "effortlessly easy," "slightly spartan." The beauty of "flabbergasted" is that it implies an astonishment that is total; I can't picture anyone being partly flabbergasted. If an action is so easy as to be effortless, use "effortless." And what is "slightly spartan"? Perhaps a monk's cell with wall-to-wall carpeting.

Don't use adverbs unless they do some work. If an athlete loses a game because he played badly, "badly" gives us the helpful information that he didn't play well. But spare us the news that he moped dejectedly and that the winner grinned widely.

ADJECTIVES. Most adjectives are also unnecessary. Like adverbs, they are sprinkled into sentences by writers who don't stop to think that the concept is already in the noun. This kind of prose is littered with precipitous cliffs and lacy spiderwebs and doleful mourners and friendly smiles. It is also littered with adjectives denoting the color of an object whose color is well known: yellow daffodils and brownish dirt. If you want to make a value judgment about daffodils, choose an adjective like "garish." If you're in a section of the country where the dirt is red, feel free to mention the red dirt. These adjectives would do a job that the noun wouldn't be doing.

Redundant adjectives are only part of the problem. Most writers sow adjectives almost unconsciously into the soil of their prose to make it more lush and pretty. The sentences become longer and longer as they fill up with stately elms and graceful boughs and frisky kittens and sleepy lagoons. This is adjective-by-habit, and it's a habit you should stop. Not every oak has to be gnarled, every detective hard-bitten. The adjective that exists solely as decoration is a self-indulgence for the writer and an obstacle for the reader.

Again, the rule is simple: make your adjectives do work that needs to be done. "He looked at the gray sky and the black clouds and decided to sail back to the harbor." The darkness of the sky is the reason for the decision. If it's important to tell the reader that a house was drab or that a girl was beautiful, by all means use "drab" and "beautiful." They will have their proper power because you have learned to use adjectives sparsely.

LITTLE QUALIFIERS. Prune out the small words that qualify how you feel and how you think and what you saw: "a bit," "a little," "sort of," "kind of," "rather," "quite," "very," "too," "pretty much" "in a very real sense," and dozens more. They dilute both your style and your persuasiveness.

Don't say you were a bit confused and sort of tired and a little depressed and somewhat annoyed. Be tired. Be confused. Be de-

pressed. Be annoyed. Don't hedge your prose with little timidities.
Good writing is lean and confident.

Don't say you weren't too happy because the hotel looked
pretty expensive. Say you weren't happy because the hotel looked
expensive. Don't tell us that you were quite fortunate. How
fortunate is that?

Don't describe an event as rather spectacular or very awesome.
Words like "spectacular" and "awesome" don't submit to measure-
ment. "Very" is a useful word to achieve emphasis, but far more
often it is clutter. There is no need to call someone very methodical. Either he is methodical or he isn't.

The larger point here is one of authority. Every little qualifier
whittles away some fraction of trust on the part of the reader. He
wants a writer who believes in himself. Don't diminish this belief.
Don't be kind of bold. Be bold.

PUNCTUATION. These are brief thoughts on punctuation, in
no way intended as a primer. If you don't know how to punctuate
—and many college students still don't—get a grammar book.

The Period. There's not much to be said about the period
except that most writers don't reach it soon enough. If you find
yourself hopelessly mired in a long sentence, it's probably because you are trying to make the sentence do more than it can
reasonably do—perhaps express two dissimilar thoughts. The
quickest way out is to break the long sentence into two short
sentences, or even three. There is no minimum length for a
sentence that is acceptable in the eyes of man and God. Among
good writers it is the short sentence that predominates, and don't
tell me about Norman Mailer—he's a genius. If you want to
write long sentences, be a genius. Or at least make sure that the
sentence is under control from beginning to end, in syntax and
punctuation, so that the reader knows where he is at every step
of the winding trail.

The Exclamation Point. Don't use it unless you must to achieve
a certain effect. It has a gushy aura—the breathless excitement
of a debutante commenting on an event that was exciting only to

her: "Daddy says I must have had too much champagne!" "But honestly, I just could have danced all night!" We have all suffered more than our share of these sentences in which an exclamation point knocks us over the head with how cute or wonderful something was. Instead, construct your sentence so that the order of the words will put the emphasis where you want it. Also resist using the exclamation point to notify the reader that you are making a joke or being ironic. "It never occurred to me that the water pistol might be loaded!" The reader is annoyed by your reminder that this was a comical moment. He is also robbed of the pleasure of making the discovery himself. Humor is best achieved by understatement, and there's nothing subtle about an exclamation point.

The Semicolon. There is a nineteenth-century mustiness that hangs over the semicolon. We associate it with the carefully balanced sentences, the judicious weighing of "on the one hand" and "on the other hand," of Conrad and Thackeray and Hardy. Therefore it should be used sparingly by writers of nonfiction today. Yet I notice that it turns up often in the excerpts that I have quoted in this book, and I have used it here myself more than I ordinarily do, mainly for the classic purpose of balancing pro and con, or of weighing two sides of the same problem. Still, the semicolon does bring the reader, if not to a halt, at least to a considerable pause. So use it with discretion, remembering that it will slow to a Victorian pace the twentieth-century momentum that you are striving for, and rely instead on the period and the dash.

The Dash. Somehow this invaluable tool is widely regarded as not quite proper—a bumpkin at the genteel dinner table of good English. But it has full membership and will get you out of many tight corners. The dash is used in two different ways. One is to amplify or justify in the second part of the sentence a thought that you have stated in the first part. "We decided to keep going—it was only 100 miles more and we could get there in time for dinner." By its very shape the dash pushes the sentence ahead and explains why they decided to keep going.

The other use involves two dashes, which set apart a parenthetical thought within a longer sentence. "She told me to get in the car—she had been after me all summer to have a haircut—and we drove silently into town." An explanatory detail that might otherwise have had to go into a separate sentence is dispatched along the way.

The Colon. The colon has begun to look even more antique than the semicolon, and many of its functions have been taken over by the dash. But it still serves well its pure role of bringing your sentence to a brief halt before you plunge into, say, a quotation or an itemized list. "The brochure said that the ship would stop at the following ports: Oran, Algiers, Naples, Brindisi, Piraeus, Istanbul and Beirut." You can't beat the colon for work like that.

MOOD CHANGERS. Learn to alert the reader as early as possible in a sentence to any change in mood from the previous sentence. At least a dozen words will do this job for you: "but," "yet," "however," "nevertheless," "still," "instead," "thus," "therefore," "meanwhile," "now," "later," "today," "subsequently" and several more. I can't overstate how much easier it is for the reader if you start with "but" when you're shifting direction, or, conversely, how much harder it is if he must wait until the end to realize that you are now in a different gear.

Many of us were taught that no sentence should begin with "but." If that's what you learned, unlearn it—there is no stronger word at the start. It announces total contrast with what has gone before, and the reader is primed for the change. If you need relief from too many sentences beginning with "but," switch to "however." It is, however, a weaker word and therefore needs careful placement. Don't start a sentence with "however"—it hangs there like a wet dishrag. And don't end with "however"— by that time it has lost its "howeverness." Put it as early as you reasonably can—as I did three sentences ago. Its abruptness then becomes a virtue.

"Yet" does almost the same job as "but," though its meaning is

closer to "nevertheless." Either of these words at the beginning
of a sentence—"Yet he decided to go" or "Nevertheless he decided
to go"—can replace a whole long phrase which summarizes what
the reader has just been told: "Despite the fact that all these
dangers had been pointed out to him, he decided to go." Look
for all the places where one of these short words will quickly
convey the same mood and meaning as a long and dismal
clause. "Instead I took the train." "Still I had to admire him."
"Thus I learned how to smoke." "It was therefore easy to meet
him." "Meanwhile I had talked to John." What a vast amount of
huffing and puffing these pivotal words save! (The exclamation
point is to show that I really mean it.)

As for "meanwhile," "now," "today" and "later," what they
also save is confusion, for writers often change their time context
without remembering to tip the reader off. "Now I know better."
"Today you can't find such an item." "Later I found out why."
Always make sure that the reader is oriented. And do it as soon
as possible whenever you change your orientation.

CONTRACTIONS. Your style will obviously be warmer and
truer to your personality if you use contractions like "I'll" and
"won't" when they fit comfortably into what you are writing. "I'll
be glad to see them if they don't get mad" is less stiff than "I will
be glad to see them if they do not get mad." There is no rule
against such informality—trust your ear and your instincts. I only
suggest avoiding one form—"I'd," "he'd," "we'd," etc.—because
"I'd" can mean both "I had" and "I would," and the reader must
often get well into a sentence before learning which meaning it
is. Frequently it turns out to be not the one he thought it was.

OVERSTATEMENT. "The living room looked as if an atomic
bomb had gone off there," writes the inexperienced writer, describing what he saw on Sunday morning after a Saturday night
party that got out of hand. Well, we all know that he's exaggerat-
ing to make a droll point, but we also know that an atomic bomb
didn't go off there, or any other bomb except maybe a water
bomb. "I felt as if ten 747 jets were flying through my brain," he

says, "and I seriously considered jumping out the window and killing myself." These verbal high jinks can get just so high— and I'm already well over the limit—before the reader feels an overpowering drowsiness. It is like being trapped with a man who can't stop reciting limericks. Don't overstate. You didn't really consider jumping out the window. Life has more than enough truly horrible funny situations. Let the humor sneak up so that we hardly hear it coming.

CREDIBILITY. The credibility of a writer is just as fragile for a writer as for a President. Don't inflate an incident to make it more flamboyant or bizarre than it actually was. If the reader catches you in just one bogus statement that you are trying to pass off as true, everything that you write thereafter will be suspect. It is too great a risk, and not worth taking.

CONCEPT NOUNS. Nouns that express a concept are commonly used in bad writing instead of verbs that tell what somebody did. Here are four typical dead sentences:
"The common reaction is incredulous laughter."
"Bemused cynicism isn't the only response to the old system."
"The anti-Establishment attitude of youth today is one reason for the tension."
"The current campus hostility is a symptom of the change."
What is so eerie about these sentences is that they have no people in them. They also have no working verbs—only "is" or "isn't." The reader can't visualize anybody performing some task. The meaning all lies in impersonal nouns that embody a vague concept: "reaction," "cynicism," "response," "attitude," "hostility." Turn these cold sentences around. Get people doing things:
"Most people just laugh with disbelief."
"Some people respond to the old system by turning cynical; others say . . ."
"One reason for the tension is that young people today feel hostile toward the Establishment."

"It's easy to notice the change—you can see how angry all the students are."

My revised sentences aren't jumping with youthful vigor, partly because the material that I'm trying to knead into shape is shapeless dough. But at least they have real people and real verbs. Don't get caught holding a bag that doesn't have anything in it but abstract nouns. You'll sink to the bottom of the lake and never be seen again.

PARAGRAPHS. Keep your paragraphs short, especially if you are writing for a newspaper or a magazine that sets its type in a narrow width. This is purely visual and psychological advice.

Short paragraphs put air around what you write and make it look inviting, whereas one long chunk of type can discourage the reader from even starting to read. A newspaper paragraph generally shouldn't have more than two or three sentences. You may worry that such frequent paragraphing will damage the logical development of your idea. (Obviously *The New Yorker* is obsessed by this fear—a reader can go for several columns without relief.) Don't worry. The gains far outweigh the dangers.

THE SUBCONSCIOUS MIND. Your subconscious mind does more writing than you think. Often you will spend a whole day trying to fight your way out of some verbal thicket in which you seem to be tangled beyond salvation. Surprisingly often a solution will occur to you the next morning when you plunge back in. While you slept, your writer's mind didn't. To some extent a writer is always working. Stay alert to the currents around you. Much of what you see and hear will come back, having percolated for days or even months through your subconscious mind, just when your conscious mind, laboring over the typewriter, needs it.

THE HUMAN CONDITION. Let's get rid of "the human condition."

14. Science

Take a class of writing students in a liberal arts college, tell them that their next assignment is to write on some aspect of science, and a pitiful moan will go around the room. "No! Not science!" the moan says. "Don't make us enter that dread region whose mysteries can only be fathomed by other scientists."

My sympathy is with them. I'm not much farther along myself than James Thurber's grandmother, who thought that "electricity was dripping invisibly all over the house" from wall sockets. But as a writer I know that a complex subject can be made as accessible to the layman as a simple subject. It's just a question of putting one sentence after another. The "after," however, is unusually important. Nowhere else must you work so hard to write sentences that form a linear sequence. This is no place for fanciful leaps or implied truths. Fact and deduction are the ruling family.

The assignment that I give to students is a seemingly primitive one. I just ask them to describe how something works. I don't care about a seductive lead or a surprise ending or any connecting devices. I only want them to tell me, say, how a sewing machine does what it does, or a bicycle, or why an apple falls down, or how the eye tells the brain what it sees. Any process will do, and science can be defined loosely to include technology, medicine and nature.

It is a tenet of journalism that "the reader knows nothing." As tenets go, it's not too complimentary, but the writer will forget it at his peril. You just can't assume that people know what you think any boob knows, or that they still remember what has once been explained to them. I doubt, for instance, if I could get into one of those life jackets that hundreds of airline stewardesses have demonstrated to me: something about pulling two toggle knobs sharply downward (or is it sideways?). I can translate the stewardesses' language—when they say "Do not effectuate these steps until you have vacated the aircraft as this will markedly increase your personal difficulty in disembarking," they mean "Don't blow the thing up or you won't get out." But what about those *other* steps—the straps that I "simply" have to slip into, the snaps I "simply" have to snap? I couldn't effectuate them if my life depended on it—as, someday, it probably will.

Describing how a process works is valuable for two reasons. First it forces you to make sure that *you* know how it works. Then it forces you to make sure that the reader will understand it as clearly as you do. In fact, I have found it to be a breakthrough assignment for many students who just couldn't disentangle themselves from vagueness, clutter and disorderly thinking.

One of them, a sophomore still immobilized in these thickets at mid-term—a bright mind spraying the page with fuzzy thoughts—was in a joyful mood when he brought me his piece on how a fire extinguisher works. I was dubious. But the piece was absolutely lucid. It explained how different kinds of fires are specifically attacked by different kinds of extinguishers. It moved with utmost simplicity and logic. I was elated by his overnight change into a writer who had learned the secret of writing sequentially. By the end of his junior year he had written and published a "how to" book that has sold better than any book *I* ever wrote, and he has now published two more that will do as well.

Many other students who were equally adrift went through the same miracle cure and have written with clarity ever since. For the principle of science writing applies to *all* nonfiction writing. It's the principle of leading a reader who knows nothing, step by step, to a grasp of the subject. Once you learn it, remember it in every article that you write.

Let me tilt the linear example by 90 degrees and ask you to imagine science writing as an upside-down pyramid. Start at the bottom with the one fact that a reader must know before he can learn any more. The second sentence broadens what was stated first, making the pyramid wider, and the third sentence broadens the second, so that gradually you can move beyond mere fact into significance and speculation—how a new discovery alters what was previously known, what new avenues of research it might open, where the research might be applied. There is no limit to how wide the inverted pyramid can become, but the reader will understand the broad implications only if he starts with a narrow fact.

A good example is an article that ran on page 1 of the *New York Times* a few years ago, by Harold M. Schmeck, Jr.

> WASHINGTON—There was a chimpanzee in California with a talent for playing ticktacktoe. Its trainers were delighted with this evidence of learning, but they were even more impressed by something else. They found they could tell from the animal's brain whether any particular move would be right or wrong. It depended on the chimpanzee's state of attention. When the trained animal was properly attentive, he made the right move.

Well, that's a reasonably interesting fact. But why is it worth page 1 of the *Times*? Paragraph 2 tells me:

> The significant fact was that scientists were able to recognize that state. By elaborate computer analysis of brain wave signals they were learning to distinguish what might be called "states of mind."

But hadn't this been possible before?

> This was far more ambitious than simply detecting gross

states of arousal, drowsiness or sleep. It was a new step toward understanding how the brain works.

How is it a new step?

The chimpanzee and the research team at the University of California at Los Angeles have graduated from the tick-tacktoe stage, but the work with brain waves is continuing. It has already revealed some surprising insights to the brain's behavior during space flight. It shows promise of application to social and domestic problems on earth and even to improvements in human learning.

Good. I could hardly ask a broader application of the research: space, human problems and the cognitive process. But is it an isolated effort? No indeed.

It is part of the large ferment of modern brain research in progress in laboratories throughout the United States and abroad. Involved are all manner of creatures from men and monkeys to rats and mice, goldfish, flatworms and Japanese quail.

I begin to see the total context. But what is the purpose?

The ultimate goal is to understand the human brain—that incredible three-pound package of tissue that can imagine the farthest reaches of the universe and the ultimate core of the atom but cannot fathom its own functioning. Each research project bites off a little piece of an immense puzzle.

So now I know where the chimp at U.C.L.A. fits into the spectrum of international science. Knowing this, I'm ready to go back and learn about his particular contribution.

In the case of the chimpanzee being taught to play tick-tacktoe, even the trained eye could see nothing beyond the ordinary in the wavy lines being traced on paper to represent electrical waves from an animal's brain. But through analysis

by computer it was possible to tell which traces showed that
the animal was about to make the right move and which
preceded a mistake.

An important key was the system of computer analysis
developed largely by Dr. John Hanley. The state of mind
that always foreshadowed a correct answer was one that
might be described as trained attentiveness. Without the
computer's ability to analyze the huge complexities of the
recorded brain waves, the "signatures" of such states could
not have been detected.

The article goes on for four columns to describe potential uses
of the research—measuring causes of domestic tension, for instance, or reducing the rush-hour stress of drivers—and eventually
it touches on work being done in many corners of the world and
in various pockets of medicine and psychology. But it started
with one chimpanzee playing ticktacktoe.

You can take much of the mystery out of science writing by
helping the reader to identify with the scientific work being done.
This means, once again, looking for the human element—and if
you have to settle for a chimpanzee, at least that's the next-
highest rung on the Darwinian ladder.

One obvious human element is yourself. Use your own experience to connect the reader to some mechanism that also touches
his life. In the following article on memory and how it operates,
which ran in *Life*, note how the writer, Will Bradbury, gives us
at the start a personal handle with which to grab an intricate
subject:

Even now I see the dark cloud of sand before it hits my
eyes, hear my father's calm voice urging me to cry the sting
away, and feel anger and humiliation burn in my chest. More
than 30 years have passed since that moment when a play-
mate, fighting for my toy ambulance, tossed a handful of
sand in my face. Yet the look of the sand and ambulance,
the sound of my father's voice and the throb of my bruised

feelings all remain sharp and clear today. They are the very first things I can remember, the first bits of visual, verbal and emotional glass imbedded in the mosaic I have come to know as *me* by what is certainly the brain's most essential function—memory.

Without this miracle function that enables us to store and recall information, the brain's crucial systems for waking and sleeping, for expressing how we feel about things and for performing complicated acts could do little more than fumble with sensory inputs of the moment. Nor would man have a real feeling of self, for he would have no gallery of the past to examine, learn from, enjoy and, when necessary, hide away in. Yet after thousands of years of theorizing, of reading and misreading his own behavioral quirks, man is just beginning to have some understanding of the mysterious process that permits him to break and store bits of passing time.

One problem has been to decide what memory is and what things have it. Linseed oil, for example, has a kind of memory. Once exposed to light, even if only briefly, it will change consistency and speed the *second* time it is exposed. It will "remember" its first encounter with the light. Electronic and fluidic circuits also have memory of a more sophisticated kind. Built into computers, they are able to store and retrieve extraordinary amounts of information. And the human body has at least four kinds of memory. . . .

That's a fine lead. Who doesn't possess some cluster of vivid images that he can recall from an inconceivably early age? The reader is eager to learn how such a feat of storage and retrieval is accomplished. The example of the linseed oil is just piquant enough to make us wonder what "memory" really is, and then the writer reverts to the human frame of reference, for it is man who has built the computer circuits and who has four kinds of memory himself.

Another method is to weave a scientific story around someone else. This is the continuing appeal of the articles called "Annals of Medicine" that Berton Roueché has long been writing in *The New Yorker*. They are detective stories, almost always involving a victim—some ordinary person struck by a mystifying ailment— and a gumshoe as obsessed as Sam Spade with finding the bacteriological villain. Here's how one of them begins:

> At about 8 o'clock on Monday morning, Sept. 25, 1944, a ragged, aimless old man of 82 collapsed on the sidewalk on Dey Street, near the Hudson Terminal. Innumerable people must have noticed him, but he lay there alone for several minutes, dazed, doubled up with abdominal cramps, and in an agony of retching. Then a policeman came along. Until the policeman bent over the old man he may have supposed that he had just a sick drunk on his hands; wanderers dropped by drink are common in that part of town in the early morning. It was not an opinion that he could have held for long. The old man's nose, lips, ears and fingers were sky-blue.

By noon, eleven blue men have been admitted to nearby hospitals. But never fear—Dr. Ottavio Pellitteri, field epidemiologist, is quickly on the scene and telephoning Dr. Morris Greenberg at the Bureau of Preventable Diseases. Slowly the two men piece together fragments of evidence that seem to defy medical history until the case is at last nailed down and the villain identified as a type of poisoning so rare that many standard texts on toxicology don't even mention it.

Roueché's secret is as old as the art of storytelling. We are in on a chase and a mystery. But he doesn't start with the medical history of poisoning, or talk about standard texts on toxicology. He gives us a man—and not only a man but a blue one.

Another way of helping the reader to understand unfamiliar scientific facts is to relate them to sights that he *is* familiar with. Reduce the abstract principle to an image that he can visualize. Moshe Safdie, the architect who conceived Habitat, the innovative housing complex at Montreal's Expo 67, explains in his book,

Beyond Habitat, that man would build better than he does if he took the time to see how nature does the job, since "nature makes form, and form is a by-product of evolution":

One can study plant and animal life, rock and crystal formations, and discover the reasons for their particular form. The nautilus has evolved so that when its shell grows, its head will not get stuck in the opening. This is known as gnomonic growth; it results in the spiral formation. It is, mathematically, the only way it can grow.

The same is true of achieving strength with a particular material. Look at the wings of a vulture, at its bone formation. A most intricate three-dimensional geometric pattern has evolved, a kind of space frame, with very thin bones that get thicker at the ends. The main survival problem for the vulture is to develop strength in the wing (which is under tremendous bending movement when the bird is flying) without building up weight, as that would limit its mobility. Through evolution the vulture has the most efficient structure one can imagine—a space frame in bone.

"For each aspect of life there are responses of form," Safdie writes, noting that the maple and the elm have wide leaves to absorb the maximum amount of sun for survival in a temperate climate, whereas the olive tree has a leaf that rotates because it must preserve moisture and can't absorb heat, and the cactus turns itself perpendicular to light. We may not know anything about botany, but we can all picture a maple leaf and a cactus plant. With every hard principle Safdie gives us a simple illustration:

Economy and survival are the two key words in nature. Examined out of context, the neck of the giraffe seems uneconomically long, but it is economical in view of the fact that most of the giraffe's food is high on the tree. . . . Beauty as we understand it, and as we admire it in nature, is never arbitrary. The color and shape of flowers directly relate to their ability to attract insects; the color and formation of insects relate to their ability to camouflage themselves against the background of flowers.

Another way of making science accessible is to write like a person and not like a scientist. It's the same old question of warmth, of being yourself. Just because you are dealing with a scholarly discipline that is usually reported in a style of dry pedantry is no reason why you shouldn't write in good fresh English. Loren Eiseley is an example of a naturalist who refuses to be cowed by his subject and is obviously enjoying himself as he passes on to us—in *The Immense Journey*—not only his knowledge but his enthusiasms:

> I have long been an admirer of the octopus. The cephalopods are very old, and they have slipped, protean, through many shapes. They are the wisest of the mollusks, and I have always felt it to be just as well for us that they never came ashore, but—there are other things that have.
>
> There is no need to be frightened. It is true that some of the creatures are odd, but I find the situation rather heartening than otherwise. It gives one a feeling of confidence to see nature still busy with experiments, still dynamic, and not through or satisfied because a Devonian fish managed to end as a two-legged character with a straw hat. There are other things brewing and growing in the oceanic vat. It pays to know this. It pays to know there is just as much future as past. The only thing that doesn't pay is to be sure of man's own part in it.

Or take this passage from *The Lives of a Cell*, by Lewis Thomas, a biologist by training but a born writer:

> A solitary ant, afield, cannot be considered to have much of anything on his mind; indeed, with only a few neurons strung together by fibers, he can't be imagined to have a mind at all, much less a thought. He is more like a ganglion on

legs. Four ants together, or ten, encircling a dead moth on a path, begin to look more like an idea. They fumble and shove, gradually moving the food toward the Hill, but as though by blind chance. It is only when you watch the dense mass of thousands of ants, crowded together around the Hill, blackening the ground, that you begin to see the whole beast, and now you observe it thinking, planning, calculating. It is an intelligence, a kind of live computer, with crawling bits for its wits.

At a stage in the construction, twigs of a certain size are needed, and all the members forage obsessively for twigs of just this size. Later, when outer walls are to be finished, thatched, the size must change, and as though given orders by telephone, all the workers shift the search to the new twigs. If you disturb the arrangement of a part of the Hill, hundreds of ants will set it vibrating, shifting, until it is put right again. Distant sources of food are somehow sensed, and long lines, like tentacles, reach out over the ground, up over walls, behind boulders, to fetch it in.

I have quoted from so many writers, writing about so many different facets of our physical world, to show that they all come across primarily as people, finding a common thread of humanity between themselves and their subject and their readers. They all write cleanly and without pretense; they all use vivid images from the vocabulary of everyday life. They aren't scared by the immensity of their subject. On the contrary, they seem to be relaxed and having a good time.

You also can achieve this rapport with your readers. Though I have used science as a demonstration model, the same principles apply to writing about any specialized field where the reader must be led across territory that is new and forbidding: business and finance, city planning and public health, government and foreign policy, architecture and agriculture. Dozens of complex professions and new technologies await the writer who can learn to describe them clearly. Only through clear writing can the rest of us ponder our future and make educated choices in areas where we have little or no education.

I'll send you away with a fragment from René Dubos' *So Human an Animal*, which won the Pulitzer Prize in 1969 for daring us to re-examine a life spent in "a confusion of concrete and steel," caught "in the midst of noise, dirt, ugliness and absurdity":

> A few years ago American scientists could state, "We *must* go to the moon, for the simple reason that we *can* do it" —echoing President John F. Kennedy, who in turn had echoed the statement by the English mountain climber George Mallory that Mount Everest *had* to be climbed, simply because it was there. Such statements are admirable to the extent that they express man's determination to accept difficult challenges, whenever and wherever there is some chance that the effort will lead to spectacular feats. But dashing expressions do not constitute an adequate substitute for the responsibility of making value judgments.
>
> There are many good scientific reasons for accepting the staggering human, financial and technological effort required to explore space and to land a man on the moon. There are equally good reasons, however, for undertaking other kinds of difficult and challenging tasks—such as exploring the earth itself or the depths of the oceans, probing into the nature of matter and energy, searching for the origins of man and his civilizations, controlling organic and mental disease, striving for world peace, eliminating city slums, preventing further desecration of nature, or dedicating ourselves to works of beauty and to the establishment of a harmonious equilibrium between man and the rest of creation.

15. Sports

I learned about the circuit clout before I learned about the electrical circuit. I also learned early—as a child addict of the sports pages—that a hurler (or twirler) who faces left when he toes the slab is a southpaw or a portsider. Southpaws were always lanky, portsiders always chunky, though I have never heard "chunky" applied to anything else except peanut butter (to distinguish it from "creamy") and I have no idea what a chunky person would look like. When hurlers fired the old horsehide, a batsman would try to solve their slants. If he succeeded he might rap a sharp bingle to the outfield, garnering a win for the home contingent, or at least knotting the count. If not, he might bounce into a twin killing, snuffing out a rally and dimming his team's hopes in the flag scramble.

I could go on, mining every sport for its lingo and extracting from the mother lode a variety of words found nowhere else in the mother tongue. Do we ever "garner" anything except a win? I could write of hoopsters and pucksters, grapplers and matmen, strapping oarsmen and gridiron standouts. I could rhapsodize about the old pigskin—far more passionately than any pig farmer —or describe the frenzied bleacherites caught up in the excitement of the autumn classic. I could, in short, write in sports English instead of good English, as if they were two different languages. Of course they're not. As in the case of writing about science or any other special subject, there is no substitute for the best.

What, you might ask, is wrong with "southpaw"? Shouldn't we be grateful for the addition to our language of a word so picturesque? Why isn't it a relief to have twirlers and circuit clouts instead of the same old pitchers and home runs? The answer is that these words have become even cheaper currency than the coins they were meant to replace. They come flooding automatically out of the typewriter of every scribe (sportswriter) in every pressbox.

The man who first thought of "southpaw" had a right to be pleased. I like to think that he allowed himself the small smile that is the due of anyone who invents a good novelty. But how long ago was that? The color that "southpaw" added to the language has paled with decades of repetition, along with the hundreds of other idioms that now form the fabric of daily sportswriting. There is a weariness about them that leaves us numb. We read the articles to find out who won, and how, but we don't read them with any real enjoyment.

The best sportswriters know this. They avoid the exhausted synonyms and strive for freshness elsewhere in the construction of a sentence. You can search the columns of Red Smith and never find a batsman bouncing into a twin killing. Smith is not afraid to let a batter hit into a double play. But you will find hundreds of unusual words—good English words—chosen with precision and fitted into situations where no other sportswriter would put them. They gratify us because the writer obviously cares about using fresh imagery in a field where his competitors settle for the same old stuff. This is why Red Smith is still in business after forty years of writing a regular column, and why his competitors have long since been sent—as they would be the first to say—to the showers.

Across the years I remember countless phrases in Red Smith's columns that took me by surprise with their humor and originality.

It was a pleasure to read about a quarterback who was "scraped off the turf like apple butter," or to be told of a seedy press conference held in "a luncheonette on 53rd Street that has long since vanished in a cloud of bicarbonate." I remember countless times when Smith, a devout angler, baited his hook and came up with that slippery fish, a sports commissioner, gasping for air.

"In most professional sports the bottom has just about dropped out of the czar business," he wrote in 1971, noting once again that the cupidity of team owners has a tendency to outrun the courage of the sport's monitors. "The first and toughest of the overlords was Kenesaw Mountain Landis, who came to power in 1920 and ruled with a heavy hand until his death in 1944. But if baseball started with Little Caesar, it wound up with Ethelred the Unready."

Or consider this column of December 2, 1974, equally lacking in reverence for the gods that a sports-loving nation has raised to Olympus:

> Tom Landry is familiar to America's television public as the tall figure wearing a hat one size too small whom they see pacing the sideline with the measured tread of a pallbearer when the Dallas Cowboys play football. Landry has watched his team win 123 games, lose 81 and tie 5 and has yet to show jubilation or disappointment. He doesn't talk much, either, but when he does speak he can be profound. "Football," he said on Thanksgiving Day, "is an incredible game. This is what makes it so unbelievable at times." You can't get much profounder than that. He was talking about the performance of a 22-year-old quarterback of towering obscurity named Clint Longley, a performance so incredible that it was practically unbelievable.
>
> Flung into a championship game for the first time in his life when Roger Staubach got the wobbles, young Longley . . . didn't know what it meant to be smacked by Diron Talbert or Chris Hamburger, so when those carnivores came thundering down on him he stood there without fear searching

for an open receiver. Just doing what comes naturally, he led a beaten team to victory and left one of the pro game's most treasured fictions shot full of holes.

This is the myth that after a college player or coach enlists with the Hessians he needs years of apprenticeship before he can hack it in the professional game. Flacks have peddled this malarky for so long in an effort to lend a spurious mystique to their product that the public now believes that the postgraduate game is to campus football as Lobachevski's geometry is to simple arithmetic. The truth is, pro football is a simplification of the undergraduate game, but we realize this only when a kid like Longley walks in from nowhere and shows us how easy it is. . . . The most timorous creature of woods or field is the professional football coach. Not daring to experiment, he imitates, plagiarizing the work of better men and reducing it to fundamentals that he can grasp.

So much for Landry and the other mental giants of his tribe. "Spurious mystique" says it in two words, but as proof Red Smith cites the various innovations in football that were created by college coaches and baldly adapted by the pros. He is the daily guardian of our perspective in a journalistic never-never land, a writer who keeps us honest. But this is largely because he is writing good English. His style is not only graceful but strong enough to carry strong convictions.

What keeps the average sportswriter from writing good English is, first, the misapprehension that he shouldn't be trying to. He has been reared on so much jargon, so many clichés, that he thinks they are the required tools of the trade.

He is also obsessed by synonyms. He has a dread of repeating the word that is easiest for the reader to visualize—batter, runner, golfer, boxer—if a synonym can be found. And usually, with exertion, it can. This excerpt from a college newspaper is typical:

> Bob Hornsby extended his skein yesterday by toppling Dartmouth's Jerry Smithers, 6-4, 6-2, to lead the netmen to

victory over a surprisingly strong foe. The gangling junior put his big serve to good use in keeping the Green captain off balance. The Memphis native was in top form as he racked up the first four games, breaking the Indian's service twice in the first four games. The Exeter graduate faltered and the Hanover mainstay rallied to cop three games. But the racquet ace was not to be denied, and Smithers' attempt to knot the first stanza at 4-4 failed when he was passed by a cross-court volley on the sixth deuce point. The redhead was simply too determined, and . . .

Whatever became of Bob Hornsby? Well might you ask. Hornsby has been metamorphosed within one paragraph into the gangling junior, the Memphis native, the Exeter graduate, the racquet ace and the redhead. The reader doesn't know him in these various disguises—or care. He only wants the clearest picture of what happened. Never be afraid to repeat the player's name and to keep the details of the game simple. A set or an inning doesn't have to be recycled into a stanza or a frame just to avoid redundancy. The cure is worse than the ailment.

Another obsession is with numbers. True, every sports addict lives with a head full of statistics, cross-filed for ready access, and many a baseball fan who once flunked simple arithmetic can perform prodigies of instant calculation in the ball park on a summer afternoon. Still, some statistics are more important than others. If a pitcher wins his twentieth game, if a golfer shoots a 61, if a runner runs the mile in 3:55, please mention it. But don't get carried away:

AUBURN, Ala., Nov. 1 (UPI)—Pat Sullivan, Auburn's sophomore quarterback, scored two touchdowns and passed for two today to hand Florida a 38-12 defeat, the first of the season for the ninth-ranked Gators.

John Reaves of Florida broke two Southeastern Conference records and tied another. The tall sophomore from Tampa, Fla., gained 369 yards passing, pushing his six-game season total to 2,115. That broke the S.E.C. season record of 2,012 set by the 1966 Heisman trophy winner, in 10 games.

Reaves attempted 66 passes—an S.E.C. record—and tied the record of 33 completions set this fall by Mississippi's Archie Manning.

Fortunately for Auburn, nine of Reaves's passes were intercepted—breaking the S.E.C. record of eight interceptions suffered by Georgia's Zeke Bratkowski against Georgia Tech in 1951.

Reaves's performance left him only a few yards short of the S.E.C. season total offense record of 2,187 set by Georgia's Frank Sinkwich in 11 games in 1942. And his two touchdown passes against Auburn left him only one touchdown pass short of the S.E.C. season record of 23 set in 1950 by Kentucky's Babe Parilli. . . .

Those are the first four paragraphs of a six-paragraph story that was prominently displayed in my New York newspaper, a long way from Auburn. It has a certain mounting hilarity—a figure freak amok at his typewriter. But can anybody read it? And does anybody care? Only Zeke Bratkowski—off the hook after twenty-odd years.

Sports is one of the richest fields now open to the nonfiction writer. Many authors better known for "serious" books have done some of their most solid work as observers of athletic combat. Many got their start in the sports section of newspapers. Gay Talese began as a sportswriter for the *New York Times*; it shows in the sensitive portrait of Joe DiMaggio that he subsequently wrote for *Esquire*. Norman Mailer's account of the Frazier-Ali fight in *Life* is one of his best pieces of writing—a psychoanalysis of boxing. John McPhee's *Levels of the Game* and George Plimpton's *Paper Lion*—one a book about tennis, the other about professional football—take us deeply into the lives of the players. In mere detail they have enough information to keep any fan happy. But what makes them special is their humanity. Who is this strange bird—the winning athlete—and what mysterious engines keep him going?

Good sportswriting is just crossing over, in fact, into whole new realms, undreamed of by the hacks who still sit in the press-box reporting the stellar exploits of chunky portsiders and Ruthian sluggers. Even Ruth has been ushered down from the sanitized slopes of Olympus and converted into a real person in *Babe*, an excellent biography by Robert W. Creamer. "The Legend Comes to Life," says the book's subtitle, which is certainly what Ruth would have wanted, hard though some of the facts may be on those who would like him to stay legendary.

The new era, incidentally, is one in which women will increasingly thrive, both as athletes entering a traditional male domain and as writers perceiving that domain as a frontier of raised consciousness. American sport has always been interwoven with social history, and the best sportswriters are those who will make the connection.

A small but pleasant example of making the connection is a small but pleasant piece by Jean Shepherd (who happens to be a man) about the Indianapolis 500. The article, which ran in the Sunday sports section of the *New York Times* in May of 1974, explains that the Indy has only one counterpart in American sport —the Kentucky Derby—and that both "can only be understood by the outsider in terms of folklore":

> Any horse that wins the Derby enters the pearly gates of history forever. Hundreds of horses have won "classics" over the years, but even non-horseplayers remember Derby winners. So it is with the 500. Who knows or cares what other races Wilbur Shaw might have won in his great career? The fact that he took the 500 three times makes him immortal.
>
> Why the Derby when there are other, richer races? A little history helps. Kentucky, with its great plantations, its soft rolling hills and lazy summers, was the true horse country of America, and 100 years ago when the Derby was born it pitted one aristocratic horse against the other. It was not just another race, but something that came out of the air and the land and the people who lived on it. . . .
>
> Indiana in the early days was to the automobile as Ken-

tucky was and is to the horse. Some of the truly great ma-
chines by any world standard were born and bred on the
Indiana flatlands. The stylish and terrifying Dusenbergs
created by the almost mythical Dusenberg brothers, Fred
and August, were hammered out a few miles from the brick
track. The Auburn, the Cord and the great racing Stude-
bakers were all spawned in dusty Indiana hamlets and came
together every spring in the dawn of automobiling to battle
it out.

The automobile also means much more to the common
people of the great plains than it does to the city folk who
huddle jammed together in the great urban East. It meant,
and still means, freedom, mobility and, above all, a way out
for lives that are often as monotonous as the landscape they
are lived in.

These are the values to look for when you write about sport:
people, places, the link between past and present, the tug of the
future. Observe closely. Hang around the track and the paddock,
the ball park and the rink. Interview in depth. Listen to old-
timers. Ponder the changes. Write well.

16. Criticism

Every writer wants at some time to be a critic. The small-town reporter dreams of the moment when his editor will summon him to cover the Russian ballet troupe, the concert pianist, the touring repertory company that has been booked into the local auditorium. Then he will trot out all the hard-won words of his college education—"intuit" and "sensibility" and "Kafkaesque"—and show the whole county that he knows a *glissando* from an *entrechat*. He will discern more symbolism in Ibsen than Ibsen ever thought of.

This is part of the urge. Criticism is the stage on which journalists do their fanciest strutting.

It is also where reputations for wit are born. The American vernacular is rich in epigrams ("She ran the gamut of emotions from A to B") minted by people like Dorothy Parker and George S. Kaufman who became famous partly by minting them, and the temptation to make an instant name at the expense of some talentless ham is too strong for all but the most saintly.

Not that the epigrams aren't enjoyable. I particularly like Kaufman's hint that Raymond Massey in *Abe Lincoln in Illinois* was perhaps overplaying the title role: "Massey won't be satisfied until he's assassinated." But true wit is rare, and a thousand barbed arrows fall at the feet of the archer for every one that flies. It is also too facile an approach if you want to write serious criticism, for, by no accident, the only epigrams that have survived are cruel ones. It is far easier to bury Caesar than to praise him—and that goes for Cleopatra, too. But to say why you think that a play is *good*, in words that don't sound banal, is one of the hardest chores in the business.

So don't be deluded that criticism is an easy route to glory or to cultural acclaim. Nor does the job carry as much power as is widely supposed. Probably only the daily drama critic of the *New York Times* can make or break the product—a new play— and a music critic has almost no power at all, writing, as he does, about a cluster of sounds that have vanished into the air and will never be heard in quite the same way again.

As for literary critics, they have never kept the best-seller list from becoming a nesting-ground for authors like Harold Robbins and Irving Wallace—whose sensibility they don't intuit—and movie critics, the most pretentious of the lot, wield almost no influence except in the case of a foreign film, where a good review can lengthen its run. You only have to compare the critics' appraisal and the box-office receipts of *The Poseidon Adventure* to see the process of non-influence in full flower. The critics judged it in artistic terms and declared it junk. But the film wasn't conceived in artistic terms—it was a movie about an ocean liner that turns upside down. It was junk, but entertaining junk.

A distinction should therefore be made between a "critic" and a "reviewer." In general a reviewer writes for a newspaper or a popular magazine, and what he covers is not primarily an art but an industry—the output of, for instance, the television industry, the motion-picture industry and, increasingly, the publishing industry in its outpouring of "gift books," cookbooks, how-to books, sex books and other such items of merchandise.

As a reviewer your job is more to report than to make an aesthetic judgment. You are the deputy for the average man or woman who wants to know: "What is the new TV series about?", "Is the movie too dirty for the kids?", "Will the book really improve my sex life or tell me how to make a chocolate mousse?" Think what *you* would want to know if *you* had to spend the money for the movie, the baby-sitter and the long-promised dinner at a good restaurant. Obviously you will make your review simpler and less sophisticated than if you were criticizing a new novel by Vladimir Nabokov.

And yet I suggest several conditions that apply equally to good reviewing and good criticism.

One is that a critic should like—or, better still, love—the medium that he is reviewing. If you think movies are dumb, don't write about them. The reader deserves a lifelong movie buff who will bring with him a reservoir of knowledge, passion and prejudice. I don't mean that the critic has to like every film. On the contrary, his prejudices are as important as his passions—criticism is, after all, only one person's opinion and a highly subjective craft. But he should go to every movie wanting to like it. If he is more often disappointed than pleased, it is because the film has failed to live up to what he knows are its best possibilities. This is far different from the critic who prides himself on hating everything, who relishes giving us his weekly dose of bile. He becomes tiresome faster than you can say Kafkaesque.

Another rule is: don't give away too much of the plot. Tell the reader just enough to let him decide whether it's the kind of story that he tends to enjoy, but not so much that you will kill his eventual enjoyment. One sentence will often do the trick. "This is a picture about a whimsical Irish priest who enlists the help of three orphan boys dressed as leprechauns to haunt a village where a mean widow has hidden a crock of gold coins." I couldn't be flailed into seeing that movie—I've had my fill of "the little people" on stage and screen. But there are legions who don't share that particular crotchet of mine and would flock to the film. Don't spoil their pleasure by revealing every twist of the narrative—especially the funny part about the troll under the bridge.

A third principle is to use as much specific detail as possible.

This avoids dealing in generalities, which, being generalities, mean nothing. "The play is always fascinating" is a typical critic's sentence. But *how* is it fascinating? Your idea of fascinating is different from the reader's. Cite a few examples and let him weigh them on his own fascination scale. Here are excerpts from two separate reviews of a film directed by Joseph Losey. (1) "In its attempts to be civilized and restrained it denies its possibilities for vulgarity and mistakes bloodlessness for taste." The sentence is vague, giving us at the most a whiff of the movie's mood but no image that we can visualize. (2) "Losey pursues a style that finds portents in lampshades and meanings in table settings." The sentence is precise—we know just what kind of arty film-making this is. We can almost see the camera lingering with studied sluggishness over the family crystal.

In book reviewing this means allowing the author's words to do their own documentation. Don't say, for instance, that Tom Wolfe's style is gaudy and unusual. Quote a few of his gaudy and unusual sentences and let the reader see how distinctive they are, how quirky. In reviewing a play, don't just tell us that the set is "striking." Describe its various levels, or how it is ingeniously lit, or how it helps the actors to make their entrances and exits as a less imaginative set would not. Put the reader in your theater seat. Help him to see what you saw.

A final caution is to avoid the ecstatic adjectives that occupy such disproportionate space in every critic's quiver—words like "enthralling" and "luminous." Good criticism needs a lean and vivid style to express what you observed and what you think. Florid adjectives smack of the panting prose with which *Vogue* likes to disclose its latest chichi discovery: "We've just heard about the most utterly enchanting little beach at Cozumel."

So much for reviewing and the simpler rules of the game. What, then, is criticism?

Criticism is a serious intellectual act. It tries to appraise serious works of art and to place them in the context of what has been done before in that medium or by that particular artist. This doesn't mean that the critic must limit himself to the work of men and women whose aims are high; he may select some commercial product like "All in the Family" to make a point about American taste and values. But on the whole he doesn't want to waste his time on peddlers. He sees himself as a scholar, and what interests him is the play of ideas in his field.

Therefore if you want to be a critic, steep yourself in the literature of the medium that you hope to make your province. If your goal is to be a theater critic, see every possible play—the good and the bad, the old and the new. Catch up on the past by reading the classics or seeing them in revival. Know your Shakespeare and Shaw, your Chekhov and Molière, your Arthur Miller and Tennessee Williams, and know what they meant to audiences of their era and how they broke new ground. Know the history of the American musical: the distinctive contribution of Jerome Kern and the Gershwin brothers, of Cole Porter, of Rodgers and Hart and Hammerstein, of Agnes DeMille and Jerome Robbins. Learn everything you can about the great actors and directors and how their methods differed, and about the great clowns like Bert Lahr. Only then can you place every new drama within an older tradition, recognize genius when it comes along and tell the pioneer from the imitator.

I could make the same kind of list for every art. A film critic who reviews a new Fellini picture without having seen most of Fellini's earlier films is not much help to the serious movie-goer. A music critic should know not only his Bach and Palestrina, his Mozart and Beethoven, but his Schoenberg and Satie, his Ives and Varèse—the theoreticians and mavericks and electronic experimenters.

Obviously I am now also assuming a more urbane body of readers. As a critic you can presuppose certain shared areas of knowledge with the men and women you are writing for. You don't have to tell them that William Faulkner was a Southern novelist. What you *do* have to do, if you are assessing the first novel of a Southern author and weighing Faulkner's influence, is to generate a provocative idea and to throw it onto the page where your fellow scholars can savor it. They may disagree with your point—that's part of their intellectual fun. But at least they have enjoyed the turn of your mind and the journey that took you to your conclusion. We like a good critic as much for his personality as for his opinions.

Let me take you traveling with a great film critic, James Agee, as he reveals what he liked best about Laurence Olivier's *Henry V*.

Some people, using I wonder what kind of dry ice for comfort, insist that *Henry V* is relatively uninteresting Shakespeare. [But] after hearing it, in this production, I find it as hard to judge fairly even the best writing since Shakespeare as it is to see the objects in a room after looking into the sun.

The one great glory of the film is this language. The greatest credit I can assign to those who made the film is that they have loved and served the language so well. I don't feel that much of the delivery is inspired; it is merely so good, so right, that the words set loose in the graciously designed world of the screen, like so many uncaged birds, fully enjoy and take care of themselves. Neither of the grimmest Shakespearean vices is indulged: none of the text is read in that human, down-to-earth, poetry-is-only-hopped-up-prose manner which is doubtless only proper when a charter subscriber to "PM" reads the [Max] Lerner editorial to his shop-wise fellow traveler; nor is any of it intoned in the nobler manner, as if by a spoiled deacon celebrating the Black Mass down a section of sewerpipe. Most of it is merely spoken by people who know and love poetry as poetry and have spent a lifetime learning how to speak it accordingly. Their voices, faces and bodies are all in charge of a man who has selected them as shrewdly as a good orchestrator selects and blends his instruments; and he combines and directs them as a good conductor conducts an orchestral piece. It is, in fact, no surprise to learn that Mr. Olivier is fond of music. Charming as it is to look at, the film is essentially less visual than musical.

Most of us remember *Henry V* for its beauty, its color, its robust vitality. Agee reminds us that it was built on still sturdier pillars. He also tells us a great deal about himself. How could we not take pleasure in a mind both so finely tuned to poetry and so impatient with the grandiose?

Turning to another medium, but to a mind no less original, here is an excerpt from *Living-Room War* by Michael J. Arlen. The book is a collection of the critical columns on television that Arlen wrote for *The New Yorker* during the viewing year of 1966–67—a year that must have taxed his retina but didn't numb his brain:

> Vietnam is often referred to as "television's war," in the sense that this is the first war that has been brought to the people preponderantly by television. People indeed look at television. They really look at it. They look at Dick Van Dyke and become his friend. They look at thoughtful Chet Huntley and find him thoughtful, and at witty David Brinkley and find him witty. They look at Vietnam. They look at Vietnam, it seems, as a child kneeling in the corridor, his eye to the keyhole, looks at two grownups arguing in a locked room—the aperture of the keyhole small; the figures shadowy, mostly out of sight; the voices indistinct, isolated threats without meaning; isolated glimpses, part of an elbow, a man's jacket (who is the man?), part of a face, a woman's face. Ah, she is crying. One sees the tears. (The voices continue indistinctly.) One counts the tears. Two tears. Three tears. Two bombing raids. Four seek-and-destroy missions. Six administration pronouncements. Such a fine-looking woman. One searches in vain for the other grownup, but, ah, the keyhole is so small, he is somewhere never in the line of sight. Look! There is General Ky. Look! There are some planes returning safely to the *Ticonderoga*. I wonder (some-

times) what it is that the people who run television think about the war, because *they* have given us this keyhole view; we have given them the airwaves, and now, at this crucial time, they have given back to us this keyhole view—and I wonder if they truly think that those isolated glimpses of elbow, face, a swirl of dress (who *is* that other person anyway?) are all that we children can stand to see of what is going on inside the room.

This is criticism at its best: stylish, allusive, disturbing. It disturbs us—as criticism often should—because it jogs a firmly held set of beliefs and forces us to re-examine them. What holds our attention here is the metaphor of the keyhole, so exact and yet so mysterious. But what remains is a fundamental question about how a country's most powerful medium tells the country's people about the war that they are fighting—and escalating. Remember that the column ran in 1966 when most Americans still supported the Vietnam war. Would they have turned against it sooner if TV had widened the keyhole, had shown us not only "the swirl of dress" but the severed head and the burning child? It is too late now to know. But at least one critic was keeping watch. Critics should always be among the first to notify us when the truths that we hold to be self-evident cease to be true.

Some arts, of course, are harder to catch in print than others. One is dance, which consists of movement. How can a writer freeze all the graceful leaps and pirouettes? Another is music. It is an art that we receive through our ears, yet the writer is stuck with describing it in words that we will see. At best he can only partly succeed, and many a music critic has built a long career by hiding from his readers behind a hedge of Italian technical terms. He will find just a shade too much *rubato* in a pianist, a tinge of shrillness in a soprano's *tessitura.*

But even in this world of evanescent notes a good critic can make sense of what happened by writing good English and by using references that mere mortals can understand. Virgil

Thomson, whose columns ran in the *New York Herald Tribune* from 1940 to 1954, was an elegant practitioner. A composer himself, an erudite and cultivated man, he still never forgot that his readers were real people, and he wrote with a zest that swept them along, his style alive with pleasant surprises. He also never forgot that musicians are real people, and he didn't hesitate to shrink the giants to human scale. What other critic would dare to secularize the sainted Toscanini?

> It is extraordinary how little musicians discuss among themselves Toscanini's rightness or wrongness about matters of speed and rhythm and the tonal amenities. Like other musicians, he is frequently apt about these and as frequently in error. What seems to be more important is his unvarying ability to put over a piece. He quite shamelessly whips up the tempo and sacrifices clarity and ignores a basic rhythm, just making the music, like his baton, go round and round, if he finds his audience's attention tending to waver. No piece has to mean anything specific; every piece has to provoke from its hearers a spontaneous vote of acceptance. This is what I call the "wow technique."

No *rubatos* or *tessituras* there, and no blind hero-worship. Yet the paragraph catches the essence of what made Toscanini great —an extra helping of showbiz. If his worshipers are offended to think that the essence contained so coarse an ingredient, they can continue to admire the Maestro for his "lyrical colorations" or "orchestral *tuttis*." I'll go along with Thomson's diagnosis, and so, I suspect, would the Maestro.

Here's another column by Virgil Thomson (a lead paragraph) which beguiles us instantly with its civility and charm:

> One has known New York men who always had their suits made in Boston and elderly ladies from various parts of the Eastern seaboard who would never go anywhere else for a hat. Certainly we do not produce here [in New York] or import from any other provincial center such perfect musical

tailoring as that which the Boston Symphony Orchestra ex-
hibits for us in Carnegie Hall ten times a season and which
was again displayed yesterday afternoon.

Finally, here is Thomson analyzing pure musicianship, telling
us why a piano recital by Josef Lhevinne was not only perfect
in itself but significantly better than the work of other major
artists:

> Any authoritative execution derives as much of its excel-
> lence from what the artist does not do as from what he does.
> If he doesn't do anything off color at all, he is correctly said
> to have taste. Mr. Lhevinne's taste is as authoritative as his
> technical method. Not one sectarian interpretation, not one
> personal fancy, not one stroke below the belt, not a sliver of
> ham, mars the universal acceptability of his readings. Every-
> thing he does is right and clear and complete. Everything
> he doesn't do is the whole list of all the things that mar the
> musical executions of lesser men.

All but one of these snippets from Agee, Arlen and Thomson
were snipped from the middle of longer columns. They therefore
don't demonstrate how a piece of good criticism should start.
Here again you must orient the reader to the specialized world
that he is about to enter. Even if he is a broadly educated person
he needs to be told or reminded of certain facts. You can't just
throw him into the water and expect him to swim easily. The
water needs some warming up.

Notice how the following review of *Virginia Woolf*, a biography
by Quentin Bell—from the *New York Times Book Review*—
begins by summarizing the main details that we should know
about Mrs. Woolf, about her paradoxical position in the world of
letters, about her biographer and about her girlhood. Not until we
possess this general information are we ready or interested enough
to follow the critic, Michael Rosenthal, down more specific and
scholarly paths.

Generally regarded as a genius by those who knew her, Virginia Woolf has long suffered from both the uncritical adulation and the virulent antipathy that genius frequently inspires. Lost in the conflict between those who worship at the altar of her sensitivity and those who decry her as snobbish, desiccated and irrelevant is any substantial notion of who Virginia Woolf actually was. Quentin Bell brings an impressive set of intellectual and genetic credentials to the task of unraveling the enigma of the "high priestess of Bloomsbury." As the son of Clive and Vanessa Bell and the nephew of Virginia, Bell would seem to be the most qualified person to reveal the facts of her life. An art critic of as much substance but less influence than his father, he has previously written a slim volume evaluating the Bloomsbury circle in which he grew up, and it was no surprise that Leonard Woolf, Virginia's husband, should have encouraged Bell to undertake the authorized biography. The results are in many ways startling.

The stage is well set. The final word, "startling," compels us to go on. How is the book startling?

Born in 1882, Virginia was the third of four children that Julia Duckworth Stephen, a young widow with three children of her own, presented Sir Leslie Stephen, the eminent Victorian whose sober rationalism and incessant self-pitying are immortalized in Mr. Ramsay of *To the Lighthouse*. The Stephen household was in fact very much like the Ramsays'; nourished by the warmth and compassion of their mother, the seven children regarded the austere Sir Leslie with proper Victorian respect. But although there were certain emotional disadvantages in having for a father the man who in addition to editing the monumental "Dictionary of National Biography" managed to produce 15 assorted volumes of history, biography and criticism and well over 100 long articles, there were a number of benefits as well.

Virginia grew up in an atmosphere densely packed with
words, ideas and, above all, books. . . .

It sounds normal enough—a respectable upper-middle-class
Victorian brood "clothed in the mantle of propriety," as the
critic puts it. "But no future study of Virginia Woolf will ever be
able to look at her life in quite the same way," he continues,
and we are off into the unwrapping of layers of lurking mad-
ness and sexual exploration without which, it now seems, no
respectable upper-middle-class Victorian family was complete.
By the end of the review we see how the author's public art and
private suffering were intertwined from her childhood on, and
why suicide was the inevitable end of both. But we had to begin
with a plain set of facts.

Today criticism has many first cousins in journalism: the newspaper or magazine column, the essay, the editorial, and the essay-
review, in which a critic digresses from a particular book or
cultural phenomenon into a larger point. (Gore Vidal, Wilfrid
Sheed and John Leonard have brought this form to a high polish.)
Many of the same principles that govern good criticism go into
these columns. A political columnist, for instance, must love
politics and know its ancient, tangled threads.

But what is common to all the forms is that they consist of
personal opinion. Even the editorial that uses "we" was obviously
written by an "I." And what is crucial for you as the writer is to
express your opinion firmly. Don't cancel its strength with last-
minute evasions and escapes. The most boring sentence in the
daily newspaper is the last sentence of the editorial, which says
that "it is still too early to tell whether the new policy will work"
or that "the effectiveness of the decision remains to be seen." If
it is still too early to tell, don't bother us with it at all, and as for
what remains to be seen, *everything* remains to be seen, including
what you will do ten minutes from now. Take your stand with
conviction.

Many years ago when I was writing editorials for the *New
York Herald Tribune*, the editor of the page was a huge and

ungainly man from Texas. I respected him because he had no pretense and because he hated any undue circling around a subject. Every morning we would all discuss what editorials we would like to write for the next day and what position we would take. Frequently we weren't quite sure, especially the writer who was an expert on Latin America.

"What about that coup in Uruguay?" the editor would ask.

"It could represent progress for the economy," the writer would reply, "or then again it might destabilize the whole political situation. I suppose I could mention the possible benefits and then . . ."

"Well," the man from Texas would break in, "let's not go peeing down both legs."

It was a plea that he made often, and it was perhaps the most inelegant advice I ever received. But over a long career of writing reviews and columns and trying to make a point that I felt strongly about, it was also probably the best.

17. Humor

Humor is the secret weapon of the nonfiction writer. It is secret because so few writers realize that it is often their best tool—and sometimes their only tool—for making an important point.

If this strikes you as a paradox, you are not alone. The professional writer of humor lives with the knowledge that half of his readers never know what he is trying to do. I remember a reporter calling to ask how I happened to write a certain parody in *Life*. At the end he said, "Should I refer to you as a humorist? Or have you also written anything serious?"

The answer, of course, is that if you're trying to write humor, almost everything that you do is serious. Few Americans understand this. We dismiss our humorists as triflers because they have never settled down to "real" work. So our Pulitzer Prizes and other awards go to authors like Ernest Hemingway and William Faulkner who are (God knows) serious and are therefore certified as men of literature. The prizes have never gone to people like George Ade, H. L. Mencken, Ring Lardner, Robert Benchley, S. J. Perelman (my own hero), Art Buchwald, Jules Feiffer and Woody Allen, who seem to be just fooling around.

They're not just fooling around. They are as serious in purpose as the Saul Bellows—in fact, a national asset in forcing the country to see itself clearly. To them humor is urgent work. It's an attempt to say important things in a special way that regular writers aren't getting said in a regular way—or, if they are, it's so regular that nobody is reading it.

One cartoon by Herblock or Bill Mauldin is worth a hundred solemn editorials. One "Doonesbury" comic strip by Garry Trudeau—a prison warden begging Jeb Magruder to stop playing squash long enough to answer a few reporters' questions about morality—is worth a hundred sober columns on our unequal penal system. One pop art painting of our neon and billboard landscape is worth a hundred earnest pieces deploring urban sprawl; it takes us by surprise and says "Look again!" One record by Arlo Guthrie, "Alice's Restaurant," is worth a hundred stern articles on the erosion of civil liberties and on what was called "law and order" until the hawkers of that phrase turned out to be unlawful and disorderly. It was one of the best pieces of topical humor to come out of the 1960's.

One *Catch-22* or *Dr. Strangelove* is more important than all the books and movies that try to show war "as it is." We're dulled by seeing war as it is—we saw it for so long on nightly TV that we no longer see it at all. But who can forget *Catch-22* or *Dr. Strangelove*—two works of comic imagination, but still the standard points of reference for anyone trying to warn us about the military mentality that could blow us all up tomorrow? Joseph Heller and Stanley Kubrick heightened the truth about war just enough to catch its essential lunacy, and we recognize it as lunacy. The joke is no joke.

This heightening of some crazy truth—to a level where it will be seen as crazy—is at the heart of what the serious humorist is trying to do. I'll give you an example that may help to explain how he goes about his mysterious work.

One day in the early 1960's I realized that suddenly half the girls and women in America were wearing haircurlers. It was of course an incredible new blight, and it was puzzling because I couldn't imagine when the girls took the curlers out. There was no evidence that they ever did. They wore them to the supermarket and to the movies and to church, and on dates, and quite

possibly to their own weddings, and to many other places where
they would be seen by many people. So what was the wonderful
event for which they were saving the wonderful hairdo that would
result from wearing all these fantastic wires?

I tried for a year to think of a way to write about this
phenomenon—to make some comment that wouldn't sound
pompous. I could have come right out and said "It's an outrage,"
"It's a national disgrace" and "Have these women no pride?" But
that would have been a sermon, and sermons are the death of
humor. The writer must find some comic device—satire, parody,
irony, lampoon, nonsense—that he can use to disguise his serious
point. Very often he never finds it, because it's hard to find, and
the point doesn't get made.

Luckily, in this case my vigil was at last rewarded. I was
browsing at my local newsstand and saw four magazines side by
side: *Hairdo, Celebrity Hairdo, Combout* and *Pouf.* I bought
all four—to the alarm of my newsdealer—and found that there
exists a whole thriving world of journalism devoted solely to hair:
life from the neck up, but not including the brain. The magazines
had hundreds of diagrams of elaborate roller positions, and they
also had lengthy columns in which a girl could send her roller
problem to the editors for their advice. This was what I had
needed. I invented a magazine called *Haircurl* and wrote a
series of parody letters and replies. The piece ran in *Life* and it
began like this:

Dear Haircurl:

I am 15 and am considered pretty in my group. I wear
baby pink rollers, jumbo size. I have been going steady with a
certain boy for 2½ years and he has never seen me without my
rollers. The other night I took them off and we had a terrible
fight. "Your head looks small," he told me. He called me a
dwarf and said I had misled him. How can I win him back?

HEARTSICK
Speonk, N.Y.

Dear Heartsick:

You have only yourself to blame for doing something so stupid. The latest "Haircurl" survey shows that 94% of American girls now wear rollers in their hair 21.6 hours a day and 359 days a year. You tried to be different and you lost your fella. Take our advice and get some super-jumbo rollers (they come in your favorite baby pink shade, too) and your head will look bigger than ever and twice as lovely. Don't ever take them off again.

Dear Haircurl:

My problem is an intimate one, but I'm so upset that I just have to ask your advice. My boyfriend likes to run his fingers through my hair. The trouble is he keeps getting them pinched in my rollers. The other night a terribly embarrassing episode happened. We were at the movies and somehow my boyfriend got two of his fingers caught (it was right where the medium roller meets the clip-curl) and couldn't get them out. I felt very conspicuous leaving the theater with his hand still in my hair, and going home on the bus several people gave us "funny looks." Fortunately I was able to reach my stylist at home and he came right over with his tools and got poor Jerry loose. Jerry was very mad and said he's not going to date me again until I get some rollers that don't have this particular habit. I think he is being unfair, but he "means business." Can you help me?

FRANTIC
Buffalo

Dear Frantic Buffalo:

We're sorry to have to tell you that no rollers have yet been developed that do not occasionally catch the fingers of boys who tousle. The roller industry, however, is working very hard on the problem, as this complaint frequently comes up. Meanwhile why not ask Jerry to wear mittens? That way you'll be happy and he'll be safe.

There were many more, and perhaps the article even made a small contribution to Lady Bird's beautification program. But the point is this: once you've read that article you can never look at haircurlers again in quite the same way. You have been jolted by humor into looking with a fresh eye at something ludicrous in our daily environment that was previously taken for granted. This is what the serious humorist is basically trying to do. The subject here isn't important—haircurlers certainly won't be the ruin of our society. But the method will work for subjects that *are* important, or for almost any subject, if you are lucky enough to find the right comic frame.

Over the last five years of *Life*, 1968–1972, I used humor to get at all kinds of subjects that might seem highly improbable. One was the petty squabbling over the shape of the table at the Vietnam peace conference in Paris. The situation had become so outrageous after nine weeks that it could only be approached through high ridicule, and I described various efforts to get peace at my own dinner table by changing its shape every night, or by lowering the chairs of different people to give them less "status," or by turning their chairs around so that the rest of us wouldn't have to "recognize" them. It was absurd, but hardly any more absurd than what was happening in Paris.

I used humor to deal with various excesses of military power. There was the time when the Atomic Energy Commission announced—in a story which ran in the Travel and Resorts section of the Sunday *New York Times*, nestled among ads for Caribbean cruises and Riviera nights—that tourists would be able to observe nuclear tests when the A.E.C. opened its new underground test site north of Las Vegas. It said that a megaton shot could make the ground shudder twelve miles away and that with luck a sightseer might see a "miles-wide curtain of dust sent up from the desert floor" and "a spectacular surface cave-in caused by huge caverns blasted underground." As I wrote in my piece, our nuclear arsenal has somehow crossed over from the realm of American defense to the realm of American leisure—a fun facility for Dad, Mom and the kids. "Undecided about your vacation? Already done Disneyland? Why not go to Nevada for the blasts?"

Then there was the week when President Nixon invaded Cambodia after seeing the movie *Patton* three times. He "identified" with Patton as a man who acted boldly in a crisis. I wrote a column listing other movies that I hoped Nixon wouldn't see, like *The Ten Commandments*. And *Moby Dick* and *Samson and Delilah*.

I used humor often to mock the pomposity of American business. In 1970, for instance, I invented the National Refractory & Brake Company and wrote a parody of its annual report, which began:

> 1969 was a year of adjustment for your company. The general slowdown in the American economy resulted in a softening of demand for the products of the National Refractory & Brake Company and a consequent reduction in worldwide unit sales. Unexpectedly high start-up costs were also incurred—notably, in the prototype development of sophisticated capacitors—which contributed to a marked reversal of anticipated gains. . . .
>
> Major changes were made in the executive structure of N. R. & B. during the fourth quarter when it was realized that greater top-management depth and flexibility would be required to meet the sharp competitive challenges of the future. Roger S. Bassinger, who became chairman and chief executive officer on January 12, 1969, resigned on October 3, 1969, for reasons of health. His resignation was accepted with an expression of appreciation for his service to the company, which he joined in 1932 as a flocculating technician. At the same time, Carl M. Baxter, president, and Victor L. Morrissey, Jr., executive vice-president for production and finance, were appointed to newly-created posts in Gabon and Malaysia, respectively, where they will explore long-term development opportunities for your company in the emerging nations.

Anybody who has ever received an annual report—and fifty million Americans do—will recognize this as one of the most distinctive styles in our language, the art of obfuscation raised high. Rich in bombast, vague in terminology, it bathes the stockholder in a glow of pleasure at having his money in a firm so healthy and responsive, whereas in fact the company often had a terrible year and was being run by boobs.

What makes my piece work as parody is that it sticks close to the form that it is parodying. Humor may seem to be an act of exaggeration, of grossly inflating the truth to get a laugh. But the "Annual Report" wouldn't succeed if it used comical names like Throckmorton and if it didn't use real phrases like "softening of demand" and "high start-up costs." Nor would the haircurler letters succeed if we didn't recognize them as a specific journalistic form, both in their style and in their mentality.

Control is vital to humor. Learn to throw away more laughs than you keep. Don't repeat the same kind of joke two or three times just to amuse the reader—he will enjoy himself more if you only make it once. Trust the sophistication of the readers who *do* know what you're doing, and don't worry about the rest.

The columns that I wrote for *Life* made people laugh. But they all had a serious purpose, which was to say: "Something grotesque is going on here—some erosion in the quality of life, or some threat to life itself, and yet everyone assumes that it's normal." Today in America the outlandish becomes routine overnight. The humorist is trying to say that it really is still outlandish.

I remember a cartoon by Bill Mauldin during the student turmoil of the late 1960's, when infantrymen and tanks were summoned to keep peace at a college in North Carolina and undergraduates at Berkeley were dispersed by a helicopter spraying them with Mace. The cartoon showed a mother pleading with her son's draft board: "He's an only child—please get him off the campus." It was Mauldin's way of pinning down this particular lunacy, and he was right on target. In fact, he was at the center of the bullseye, as Kent State and Jackson State subsequently proved. Obviously the targets will change from week to week and from year to year. But there will never be a dearth of new lunacies—and dangers—for the humorist to detect and to fight. Lyndon Johnson in the years of his Vietnamization was brought down partly by Jules Feiffer and Art Buchwald. Joseph McCarthy and Spiro Agnew were brought down partly by Walt Kelly in the comic strip *Pogo*. H. L. Mencken brought down a whole galaxy of hypocrites in high places, and "Boss" Tweed was partly toppled by the cartoons of Thomas Nast.

Mort Sahl, a comic, was the only person who stayed awake during the Eisenhower years when all of America was under sedation and didn't want to be roused. Of the suddenly-revealed missile gap he said: "Maybe the Russians will steal all our secrets —then *they'll* be two years behind." When the House Un-American Activities Committee was at its most virulent, he said: "Every time the Russians throw an American in jail, the Committee throws an American in jail to get even."

Many people regarded Sahl as a cynic, but he thought of himself as an idealist. "If I criticize somebody," he said, "it's because I have higher hopes for the world, something good to replace the bad. I'm not saying what the Beat Generation says: 'Go away because I'm not involved.' I'm here and I'm involved."

"I'm here and I'm involved"—make this your creed if you seriously want to write serious humor. The humorist operates on a deeper current than most people suspect. He must not only make a strong point; he must be willing to go against the grain, to state what the populace and the Presidents may not want to hear. Herblock and Art Buchwald perform an act of courage at least once a week. They say things which need to be said but which a "serious" columnist couldn't get away with. What saves them is that politicians are not known for humor and are therefore even more befuddled by it than the citizenry. As Buchwald once explained: "Some of my inside sources tell me that President Johnson reads me and chuckles. Other equally informed sources tell me that he does not read me. I suspect that the truth lies somewhere in between: he reads me but does not chuckle."

It is a lonely and perilous calling. No other kind of writer risks his neck so visibly or so often on the high wire of public approval. It is the thinnest wire in all nonfiction, and the humorist knows that he will frequently fall off. Yet he is in dead earnest, this acrobat bobbing over our heads, trying to startle us with nonsense into seeing our lives with sense.

Sources

Most of the material by other writers that I have quoted in these pages was first written for a magazine or a newspaper and was subsequently reprinted in a book. In general the source cited below is for the original hardcover edition of the book. Many of these editions are now out of print but are available in public libraries. In many other cases the book has been reprinted in paperback and is relatively easy to obtain.

As for the body of this book, it was written to be what it is— an informal textbook for students and laymen—and is not a collection of articles that have previously appeared. One exception is Chapter 7, which has been adapted from my article, "Is It an O.K. Word, Usewise?", which first ran in *Life* on Aug. 24, 1969.

P. 24—Preface by E. B. White to *A Basic Chicken Guide* by Roy E. Jones. Copyright 1944 by Roy E. Jones. Reprinted by permission of William Morrow & Co. Also appears in *The Second Tree from the Corner*. Harper & Bros., 1954.

P. 24—"The Hills of Zion," by H. L. Mencken, from *The Vintage Mencken*, gathered by Alistair Cooke. Vintage Books (paper), 1955.

P. 27—*Fear and Loathing in Las Vegas*, by Hunter S. Thompson. Random House, 1972.

P. 31—"Skorpios," by Paul O'Neil. *Life*, Nov. 1, 1968. © 1968, Time Inc. Reprinted with permission.

P. 34—*Here Is New York*, by E. B. White. Harper & Bros., 1949.

P. 52—*The Lunacy Boom*, by William Zinsser. Harper & Row, 1970.

P. 54—*Pop Goes America*, by William Zinsser, Harper & Row, 1966.

P. 55—*The Lunacy Boom.*

P. 57—*Slouching Towards Bethlehem*, by Joan Didion. Farrar, Straus & Giroux, 1968, Copyright © 1966 by Joan Didion. Reprinted by permission of the publisher.

P. 59—*Nixon Agonistes*, by Garry Wills. Houghton Mifflin, 1970. Reprinted by permission of the publisher.

P. 60—"The Last Time I Played Rugby," by Richard Burton. From *The Observer* (London), Oct. 4, 1970.

P. 64—*Nixon Agonistes*, by Garry Wills.

P. 65—"Coolidge," by H. L. Mencken, from *The Vintage Mencken.*

P. 66—*Pop Goes America*, by William Zinsser.

P. 78—*The Bottom of the Harbor*, by Joseph Mitchell. Little, Brown and Company, 1960. Reprinted by permission of Harold Ober Associates, Incorporated. © 1960 by Joseph Mitchell.

P. 84—*Slouching Towards Bethlehem*, by Joan Didion.

P. 85—*A Walker in the City*, by Alfred Kazin. Harcourt, Brace, 1951.

P. 87—*No Room in the Ark*, by Alan Moorehead. Originally appeared in *The New Yorker* and reprinted by permission of Harper & Row, Publishers, Inc.

P. 89—*The Offensive Traveller*, by V. S. Pritchett. Alfred A. Knopf, 1964.

P. 91—*Of a Fire on the Moon*, by Norman Mailer. Little, Brown and Company, 1971. © 1969, 1970 by Norman Mailer. By permission of the publisher.

P. 104—"Brain Signals in Test Foretell Action," Feb. 13, 1971, by Harold M. Schmeck, Jr. © 1971 by the New York Times Company. Reprinted by permission.

P. 106—"The Mystery of Memory," by Will Bradbury. *Life*, Nov. 12, 1971. © 1971, Time Inc. Reprinted with permission.

P. 108—*Eleven Blue Men and Other Narratives of Medical Detection*, by Berton Roueché. Little, Brown and Company, 1954.

P. 109—*Beyond Habitat*, by Moshe Safdie. The M.I.T. Press, 1970.

P. 110—*The Immense Journey*, by Loren Eiseley. Random House, 1957.

P. 110—*The Lives of a Cell: Notes of a Biology Watcher*, by Lewis Thomas. Viking Press, 1974.

P. 112—*So Human an Animal*, by René Dubos. Charles Scribner's Sons, 1968.

P. 115—"Pro Football's Spurious Mystique," Dec. 2, 1974, by Red Smith.

P. 119—"In Indiana, The Roar of the Motor is the Sweetest Sound," May 26, 1974, by Jean Shepherd. Both © 1974 by the New York Times Company. Reprinted by permission.

P. 126—*Agee on Film*, by James Agee. McDowell Obolensky, 1958.

P. 127—*Living-Room War*, by Michael J. Arlen. Viking Press, 1969.

P. 129—*The Musical Scene*, by Virgil Thomson. Alfred A. Knopf, 1945.

P. 130—*Ibid.*

P. 131—"Virginia Woolf," Nov. 5, 1972, by Michael Rosenthal. © 1972 by the New York Times Company. Reprinted by permission.

P. 136—*The Haircurl Papers*, by William Zinsser. Harper & Row, 1964.

Index

147